BIBLICAL
Sudoku Puzzles

James Ormond

Paulist Press
New York/Mahwah, NJ

Cover and book design by Lynn Else

ISBN: 978-0-8091-4665-9

Published by Paulist Press
997 Macarthur Boulevard
Mahwah, New Jersey, 07430

www.paulistpress.com

Printed and bound in the
United States of America

HOW TO USE THIS BOOK

The puzzles in this book operate on the same principle as the traditional Sudoku puzzle.

There are nine boxes in each row and column and nine smaller boxes forming nine larger boxes in the complete square.

Each row and column must contain the complete phrase from the selected verse of scripture (including the book, chapter and verse references) without repeating any part of the verse within the row or any of the columns it crosses.

For example:

(LOVE)	(JUSTICE)	(YOU)	(WHO)	(JUDGE)	(THE)	(EARTH)	(WIS)	(1:1)
1	2	3	4	5	6	7	8	9

Similarly, each of the nine larger boxes in the puzzle must also contain the complete verse phrase (including the book, chapter and verse references) without any duplication while also adhering to the rule outlined above.

When two words are used in one box, they are underlined in the scripture verse. When the scripture reference is used together or broken up, that is underlined in the verse as well.

The answer key for all puzzles begins on page 93.

We hope you enjoy the challenges of each puzzle and also become familiar with the scripture passages through the process. Good luck!

		YOUR	3:2	ALL	MERCY	WAYS		
	WAYS						AND	
MERCY								
AND								
ARE				TOB	ALL	MERCY	3:2	TRUTH
TRUTH								YOUR
WAYS								3:2
	ALL						ARE	
		TOB	WAYS	MERCY	YOUR	TRUTH		

"You are righteous, O Lord, and all your deeds are just;
ALL YOUR WAYS ARE MERCY AND TRUTH;
you are the judge of the world."
TOB 3:2

MAY		YOU				BE		OF
			BE	MINDFUL	OF			
	ME	O	OF		MAY	YOU	MINDFUL	
YOU				O				LORD
	LORD	TOB 3:3	MINDFUL		BE	MAY	ME	
			YOU	MAY	LORD			
LORD		OF				ME		MINDFUL

"And now, O LORD, MAY YOU BE MINDFUL OF ME,
and look with favor upon me."
<u>TOB 3:3</u>

PUZZLE **2**

YES	AND						MANY	TRUE
YOUR		TOB				ARE		3:5
ARE			YOUR	3:5	YES			TOB
	MANY						AND	
TRUE			JUDG-MENTS	AND	3:5			MANY
AND		JUDG-MENTS				3:5		ARE
TOB			3:5	JUDG-MENTS	MANY			YES
	YES						3:5	
		YOUR	TOB	YES	TRUE	MANY		

"YES, YOUR JUDGMENTS ARE MANY AND TRUE
in dealing with me as my sins and those of my fathers deserve.
For we have not kept your commandments, nor have we
trodden the paths of truth before you."
TOB 3:5

							O	ARE
	LORD	MERCIFUL	3:11				TOB	BLESSED
	YOU		LORD					
	3:11	TOB	ARE					
				BLESSED	MERCIFUL	YOU		
				GOD		BLESSED		
ARE	BLESSED			O	3:11	GOD		
3:11	GOD							

"BLESSED ARE YOU, O LORD, MERCIFUL GOD!
Forever blessed and honored is your holy name;
may all your works forever bless you."
TOB 3:11

PUZZLE 4

					AND	I	NOW	
NOW	TO YOU	I	FACE				O LORD	
AND			NOW				MY	
TO YOU				AND		FACE	TOB 3:12	
	TURN	NOW		TOB 3:12				TO YOU
	NOW				TURN			O LORD
	O LORD				TOB 3:12	MY	I	NOW
	I	TOB 3:12	TO YOU					

"AND NOW, <u>O LORD</u>, <u>TO YOU</u> I TURN MY FACE
and raise my eyes."
<u>TOB 3:12</u>

PUZZLE **5**

		I			INNOCENT	O	AM	
				THAT				TOB 3:14
		O		KNOW				I
		AM					INNOCENT	
		THAT				MASTER		
	TOB 3:14					YOU		
INNOCENT				TOB 3:14		I		
KNOW				O				
	I	MASTER	INNOCENT			AM		

"YOU KNOW, O MASTER, THAT I AM INNOCENT
of any impure act with a man."
TOB 3:14

PUZZLE 6

THE								BREAD
	YOUR	OF	GIVE				TO	
				TO			SOME	
					HUNGRY	OF	BREAD	
	TO	GIVE	THE					
	TOB 4:16			HUNGRY				
	OF				TOB 4:16	YOUR	THE	
HUNGRY								TOB 4:16

"GIVE TO THE HUNGRY SOME OF YOUR BREAD,
and to the naked some of your clothing.
Whatever you have left over, give away as alms;
and do not begrudge the alms you give."
TOB 4:16

EXALT	13:7	FOR	ME	I	TOB	AS	MY	GOD
TOB								EXALT
AS		I	GOD	EXALT	13:7	FOR		TOB
GOD				TOB				FOR
13:7				MY				ME
MY		EXALT		FOR				I
FOR		AS	MY	ME				13:7
I							GOD	AS
ME	EXALT	13:7	TOB	GOD	AS	I	FOR	MY

"AS FOR ME, I EXALT MY GOD, and my spirit rejoices
in the King of heaven."
TOB <u>13:7</u>

PUZZLE **8**

	GOD	BLESSED				UP	TOB 13:18	
UP			GOD		BLESSED			HAS
WHO			HAS		TOB 13:18	UP		GOD
BE			RAISED		YOU			TOB 13:18
	UP	HAS	BLESSED			WHO	GOD	RAISED
			UP					BE
			YOU					UP
RAISED			BE		UP			WHO
	YOU	UP				HAS	BE	

"The gates of Jerusalem shall sing hymns of gladness,
and all her houses shall cry out, 'Alleluia!
BLESSED BE GOD WHO HAS RAISED YOU UP!
May he be blessed for all ages!' For in you they
shall praise his holy name forever."
TOB 13:18

				NEW				
			SING		TO			
		1				16:		
		16:		SING		SONG		
	SONG	NEW				A	16:	
HIM	A	TO		16:		SING	NEW	JDT
		SONG				JDT		
	TO	A	HIM		SONG	1	SING	
NEW	JDT			1			TO	SONG

"Strike up the instruments, a song to my God
with timbrels, chant to the Lord with cymbals;
SING TO HIM A NEW SONG,
exalt and acclaim his name."
JDT 16: 1

PUZZLE **10**

		MY	A NEW		HYMN	TO		
	HYMN						JDT 16:13	
GOD				TO				HYMN
I								WILL
		SING				A NEW		
JDT 16:13								TO
A NEW				JDT 16:13				GOD
	GOD						I	
		I	HYMN		MY	WILL		

"<u>A NEW</u> HYMN I WILL SING TO MY GOD.
O Lord, great are you and glorious,
wonderful in power and unsurpassable."
<u>JDT 16:13</u>

SAMARIA		AND	JDT 1:9	IN	CITIES	THOSE		TO
ITS		CITIES						JDT 1:9
JDT 1:9		THOSE	ITS	ALL	TO	CITIES		AND
TO						JDT 1:9		SAMARIA
AND		SAMARIA	TO	ITS	JDT 1:9	IN		THOSE
	JDT 1:9						AND	
		TO			AND			
			AND		IN			
THOSE				TO				

"TO ALL THOSE IN SAMARIA AND ITS CITIES,
and west of the Jordan as far as Jerusalem, Bethany,
Chelous, Kadesh, and the River of Egypt;
to Tahpanhes, Raamses, all the land of Goshen."
JDT 1:9

PUZZLE **12**

								JDT 2:7
	AND	HAVE	READY		WATER	TELL	TO	
JDT 2:7				HAVE		READY		AND
TELL			EARTH		TO			THEM
HAVE				TELL				READY
	EARTH		AND		HAVE		TELL	
TO		READY				THEM		
AND	THEM		TELL		READY			
WATER	HAVE	EARTH		TO				

"TELL THEM TO HAVE EARTH AND WATER READY,
for I will come against them in my wrath;
I will cover all the land with the feet of my soldiers,
to whom I will deliver them as spoils."
JDT 2:7

PUZZLE **13**

							RESIST	THOSE
	SHOW	THEM	JDT 2:11				QUARTER	FOR
	WHO		SHOW					
	JDT 2:11	QUARTER	THOSE					
					FOR	THEM	WHO	
					NO		FOR	
THOSE	FOR				RESIST	JDT 2:11	NO	
JDT 2:11	NO							

"As FOR THOSE WHO RESIST, SHOW THEM NO QUARTER,
but deliver them up to slaughter and plunder
in each country you occupy."
JDT 2:11

					LIKE	DUST	LOCUSTS	
LOCUSTS	THE	DUST	JDT				OR	
LIKE			LOCUSTS				EARTH	
THE				LIKE		JDT	2:20	
	OF THE	LOCUSTS		2:20				THE
	LOCUSTS				OF THE			OR
	OR				2:20	EARTH	DUST	LOCUSTS
	DUST	2:20	THE					

"A huge, irregular force, too many to count,
LIKE LOCUSTS OR THE DUST OF THE EARTH,
went along with them."
JDT 2:20

ALL								SWORD
	THE	TO	AND				PUT	
				PUT			YOUTHS	
					THEIR	TO	SWORD	
	PUT	AND	ALL					
	JDT 2:27			THEIR				
	TO				JDT 2:27	THE	ALL	
THEIR								JDT 2:27

"Descending to the plain of Damascus at the time of the wheat harvest, he set fire to all their fields, destroyed their flocks and herds, despoiled their cities, devastated their plains, AND PUT ALL THEIR YOUTHS TO THE SWORD."
JDT 2:27

PUZZLE **16**

				OF HIM				
			THE		FEAR			
		JDT 2:28				ALL		
		ALL		THE		FELL		
	FELL	OF HIM				DREAD	ALL	
AND	DREAD	FEAR		ALL		THE	OF HIM	UPON
		FELL				UPON		
	FEAR	DREAD	AND		FELL	JDT 2:28	THE	
OF HIM	UPON			JDT 2:28			FEAR	FELL

"THE FEAR AND DREAD <u>OF HIM</u> FELL UPON ALL
the inhabitants of the coastland, upon those in Sidon and Tyre, and
those who dwelt in Sur and Ocina, and the inhabitants of Jamnia.
Those in Azotus and Ascalon also feared him greatly."
<u>JDT 2:28</u>

			USE	PLEASE	YOU			
		YOU				USE		
	JDT		THEM		AS		PLEASE	
3:3		MAKE				YOU		AS
JDT				YOU				OF
PLEASE		THEM				3:3		JDT
	3:3		JDT		THEM		YOU	
		USE				AS		
			AS	OF	PLEASE			

"Our dwellings and all our wheat fields, our flocks and herds,
and all our encampments are at your disposal;
MAKE USE OF THEM AS YOU PLEASE."
JDT 3:3

PUZZLE **18**

		SEE	COME		AND	AS YOU		
	AND						JDT 3:4	
FIT				AS YOU				AND
DEAL								WITH
		THEM				COME		
JDT 3:4								AS YOU
COME				JDT 3:4				FIT
	FIT						DEAL	
		DEAL	AND		SEE	WITH		

"Our cities and their inhabitants are also at your service;
COME AND DEAL WITH THEM <u>AS YOU</u> SEE FIT."
<u>JDT 3:4</u>

			6					
	ARMY						WENT	
HE		3:	WITH		DOWN	HIS		JDT
		WITH				JDT		DOWN
			JDT					
WENT		JDT				HE		
ARMY		DOWN	HE		HIS	WENT		3:
	3:						ARMY	
				WITH				

"HE WENT DOWN WITH HIS ARMY
to the seacoast, and stationed garrisons in the fortified cities;
from them he impressed picked troops as auxiliaries."
JDT <u>3: 6</u>

GEBA			SET	BETWEEN				HIS
	UP		CAMP				3:10	
	HE		UP				JDT	
						UP	HIS	HE
UP								GEBA
HIS	CAMP	HE						
	HIS				GEBA		BETWEEN	
	SET				JDT		HE	
JDT				CAMP	UP			SET

"HE SET UP HIS CAMP BETWEEN GEBA
and Scythopolis, and stayed there a whole month to
refurbish all the equipment of his army."
JDT 3:10

OF			WERE	JDT				
	JDT	IN		OF		EXTREME	DREAD	
	THEY	HIM			DREAD	WERE	JDT	
		JDT						EXTREME
DREAD	4:2			IN			THEY	WERE
HIM				THEY		DREAD		
	OF	EXTREME	HIM			JDT	WERE	
	WERE	DREAD		EXTREME		IN	OF	
			WERE	IN				DREAD

"THEY WERE IN EXTREME DREAD OF HIM,
and greatly alarmed for Jerusalem and
the temple of the Lord, their God."
JDT 4:2

MEN	GOD	THE			OF		JDT 4:9	ALL
ALL			MEN	ISRAEL				THE
				THE				OF
			THE		MEN		GOD	
	CRIED	TO		JDT 4:9		THE	ALL	
	OF		GOD		TO			
TO				OF				
OF				GOD	CRIED			JDT 4:9
JDT 4:9	THE					CRIED	OF	ISRAEL

"ALL THE MEN OF ISRAEL CRIED TO GOD
with great fervor and did penance."
JDT 4:9

					THE	HAD		
				AND				
CRY		LORD	HAD		HEARD	JDT 4:13		
JDT 4:13		HEARD				THE		
	REGARD			THEIR			AND	
		THE				LORD		CRY
		HAD	JDT 4:13		AND	CRY		HEARD
				CRY				
		THEIR	HEARD					

"THE LORD HEARD THEIR CRY AND HAD REGARD
for their distress. For the people observed a fast of many days'
duration throughout Judea, and before the sanctuary
of the Lord Almighty in Jerusalem."
JDT 4:13

PUZZLE **24**

THEIR		LORD		THEY		ALL		STRENGTH
	CRIED		ALL		THEIR		TO THE	
STRENGTH		CRIED		THEIR		THEY		WITH
WITH		THEY		JDT 4:15		STRENGTH		LORD
	JDT 4:15		STRENGTH		LORD		THEY	
LORD		ALL		WITH		TO THE		CRIED

"With ashes upon their turbans,
THEY CRIED <u>TO THE</u> LORD WITH ALL THEIR STRENGTH
to look with favor on the whole house of Israel."
<u>JDT 4:15</u>

PUZZLE **25**

						JDT 5:2	ALL	
				RULERS	IN	GREAT		
		JDT 5:2	SUMMONED					
THE	GREAT							
ANGER								SUMMONED
							HE	ANGER
					THE	RULERS		
		SUMMONED	ANGER	GREAT				
	JDT 5:2	IN						

"IN GREAT ANGER HE SUMMONED ALL THE RULERS
of the Moabites, the generals of the Ammonites,
and all the satraps of the seacoast."
JDT 5:2

PUZZLE **26**

			HAVE		TO		THEY	WHY
		REFUSED			THEY			
JDT		WHY		REFUSED	COME			
WHY	OUT		JDT		REFUSED			
		5:4		HAVE		COME		
			TO		5:4		WHY	OUT
			THEY	WHY		5:4		JDT
			REFUSED			HAVE		
REFUSED	JDT		COME		OUT			

"WHY HAVE THEY REFUSED TO COME OUT to meet me
along with all the other inhabitants of the West?"
<u>JDT 5:4</u>

							DARK	
	IT			A			AND	
		AND		DARK			A:7	A
	GLOOMY				A:7			WAS
A:7		DAY	A	IT	WAS	ESTH		AND
WAS			AND				DAY	
A	ESTH			GLOOMY		DARK		
	WAS			A:7			IT	
	AND							

"IT WAS A DARK AND GLOOMY DAY. Tribulation and distress, evil and great confusion, lay upon the earth."
ESTH A:7

PUZZLE 28

	IS	RESIST						
	YOU	THERE		RESIST	ESTH C:4		LORD	NO ONE
				CAN	IS		YOU	RESIST
	THERE	WHO	NO ONE		CAN			
	NO ONE	IS				LORD	CAN	
			IS		RESIST	ESTH C:4	NO ONE	
YOU	RESIST		CAN	IS				
IS	WHO		LORD	THERE		CAN	RESIST	
						YOU	WHO	

"You are Lord of all, and THERE IS <u>NO ONE</u> WHO CAN RESIST YOU, LORD." <u>ESTH C:4</u>

ESTH								KING
	THE LORD		THE	AND	INVOKE		TO	
		AND	B:9		ESTH	SPEAK		
	KING	B:9				AND	THE LORD	
	ESTH			SPEAK			THE	
	SPEAK	THE				ESTH	KING	
		SPEAK	KING		TO	THE LORD		
	INVOKE		AND	THE LORD	SPEAK		B:9	
TO								AND

"INVOKE THE LORD AND SPEAK TO THE KING
for us: save us from death."
ESTH B:9

PUZZLE **30**

STOOD		WITH				KING		THE
	ESTH		THE		D:6		SHE	
	THE					FACE		
KING	WITH		FACE		TO FACE		STOOD	D:6
				D:6				
	FACE	TO FACE	STOOD	ESTH	THE	SHE	WITH	
		D:6				TO FACE		
		SHE				WITH		
			KING	STOOD	ESTH			

"She passed through all the portals till
SHE STOOD FACE <u>TO FACE</u> WITH THE KING,
who was seated on his royal throne, clothed in full
robes of state, and covered with gold and
precious stones, so that he inspired great awe."
<u>ESTH D:6</u>

THE KING						F:3		ESTHER
	WHOM		ESTHER	F:3	RIVER		IS	
ESTH			IS		THE KING			
	MARRIED	IS				THE	RIVER	
	RIVER		ESTH	IS	THE		F:3	
	ESTH	THE				ESTHER	THE KING	
		F:3		ESTH				RIVER
	THE		WHOM	THE KING	MARRIED		ESTHER	
MARRIED		WHOM						THE

"The tiny spring that grew into a river, the light of the sun, the many waters. THE RIVER IS ESTHER, WHOM THE KING MARRIED and made queen."
ESTH F:3

					FAITHFUL	TRIAL	IN	
				ABRAHAM				
	2:52	NOT	IN		TRIAL	ABRAHAM	WAS	
2:52	ABRAHAM			FAITHFUL			FOUND	WAS
TRIAL								IN
FOUND								TRIAL
1 MACC								ABRAHAM
	FOUND						NOT	
		ABRAHAM	1 MACC	TRIAL	2:52	IN		

"WAS NOT ABRAHAM FOUND FAITHFUL IN TRIAL,
and it was reputed to him as uprightness?"
1 MACC 2:52

		A		OF		1 MACC 2:62		
				A				
1 MACC 2:62			SINFUL		WORDS			DO NOT
		OF				A		
DO NOT	SINFUL			1 MACC 2:62			OF	THE
		1 MACC 2:62				MAN		
THE			MAN		OF			1 MACC 2:62
				DO NOT				
		MAN		FEAR		WORDS		

"<u>DO NOT</u> FEAR THE WORDS OF A SINFUL MAN,
for his glory ends in corruption and worms."
<u>1 MACC 2:62</u>

PUZZLE **34**

			HOLY	PEACE	PERFECT			
		PERFECT				HOLY		
	2 MACC		LIVED		IN		PEACE	
3:1		THE				PERFECT		IN
2 MACC				PERFECT				CITY
PEACE		LIVED				3:1		2 MACC
	3:1		2 MACC		LIVED		PERFECT	
		HOLY				IN		
			IN	CITY	PEACE			

"While THE HOLY CITY LIVED IN PERFECT PEACE
and the laws were strictly observed because of the piety
of the high priest Onias and his hatred of evil...."
2 MACC 3:1

				WORLD				
			LORD		OF THE			
		WIS				WORLD		
	FOR THE						1:7	
1:7	SPIRIT	OF THE	FOR THE	THE	WIS	FILLS	WORLD	LORD
	WORLD						FOR THE	
	WIS			OF THE	WORLD		SPIRIT	
	THE			FOR THE	LORD		WIS	
	LORD	WORLD	WIS	1:7	SPIRIT	OF THE	FILLS	

"FOR THE SPIRIT OF THE LORD FILLS THE WORLD,
is all-embracing, and knows what man says."
WIS 1:7

PUZZLE **36**

			1:1					
	THE						JUSTICE	
LOVE		WIS	WHO		YOU	JUDGE		EARTH
		WHO				EARTH		YOU
				EARTH				
JUSTICE		EARTH				LOVE		
THE		YOU	LOVE		JUDGE	JUSTICE		WIS
	WIS						THE	
					WHO			

"LOVE JUSTICE, YOU WHO JUDGE THE EARTH; think of the LORD in goodness, and seek him in integrity of heart."
<u>WIS 1:1</u>

WISDOM			NOT	EVIL				THAT
	A SOUL		PLOTS				WIS 1:4	
	INTO		A SOUL				ENTERS	
						A SOUL	THAT	INTO
A SOUL								WISDOM
THAT	PLOTS	INTO						
	THAT				WISDOM		EVIL	
	NOT				ENTERS		INTO	
ENTERS				PLOTS	A SOUL			NOT

"Because INTO A SOUL THAT PLOTS EVIL WISDOM ENTERS NOT, nor dwells she in a body under debt of sin."
WIS 1:4

	LIFETIME						OF	
PASSING		IS THE				OUR		A
			WIS 2:5	SHADOW	OUR			
	SHADOW		OUR		A		FOR	
	OUR	A		WIS 2:5		OF	LIFETIME	
	FOR		OF		LIFETIME		A	
			FOR	OF	PASSING			
SHADOW		FOR				LIFETIME		IS THE
	PASSING						OUR	

"FOR OUR LIFETIME IS THE PASSING OF A SHADOW;
and our dying cannot be deferred because it is fixed
with a seal; and no one returns."
WIS 2:5

MOUTH		LYING				AND		
			SLAYS					
1:11		A				SOUL		MOUTH
			THE		1:11			
	MOUTH						THE	
			AND		A			
SLAYS		1:11				A		THE
				SOUL				
		WIS				1:11		SLAYS

"Therefore guard against profitless grumbling, and from calumny withhold your tongues; For a stealthy utterance does not go unpunished, AND A LYING MOUTH SLAYS THE SOUL."
WIS 1:11

						IS	HOW	
					HIS	WIS		
	HIS			WIS	WITH			
5:5	WIS							
SAINTS								THE
							IS	LOT
		HOW	5:5				LOT	
	THE	WITH						
	WITH	HIS						

"See how he is accounted among the sons of God;
HOW HIS LOT IS WITH THE SAINTS!"
WIS 5:5

PUZZLE **41**

					SUN			
		FOR	THE	NOT		RISE		
	RISE	THE		DID			NOT	
	AND							DID
	NOT	RISE		SUN		WIS 5:6	FOR	
DID							US	
	SUN			US		DID	AND	
		NOT		FOR	AND	US		
			WIS 5:6					

"We, then, have strayed from the way of truth,
and the light of justice did not shine for us,
AND THE SUN DID NOT RISE FOR US."
<u>WIS 5:6</u>

PUZZLE **42**

	AND	NOT						
		LEARN			YOU			
					THAT			WIS 6:9
				WISDOM			WIS 6:9	THAT
THAT								YOU
WISDOM	MAY		SIN					
NOT		THAT						
		AND				MAY		
						NOT	LEARN	

"To you, therefore, O princes, are my words addressed that you may LEARN WISDOM AND THAT YOU MAY NOT SIN."
<u>WIS 6:9</u>

								WIS 8:2
	FROM	SOUGHT	YOUTH		MY	HER	AND	
WIS 8:2				SOUGHT		YOUTH		FROM
HER			AFTER		AND			I LOVED
SOUGHT				HER				YOUTH
	AFTER		FROM		SOUGHT		HER	
AND		YOUTH				I LOVED		
FROM	I LOVED		HER		YOUTH			
MY	SOUGHT	AFTER		AND				

"HER <u>I LOVED</u> AND SOUGHT AFTER FROM MY YOUTH;
I sought to take her for my bride and
was enamored of her beauty."
<u>WIS 8:2</u>

PUZZLE **44**

7:				LOVES				
THERE	28	FOR	WIS	IS			NOUGHT	
WIS				FOR				IS
FOR				28				THERE
	WIS	THERE	NOUGHT		LOVES	7:		FOR
		IS					28	
		WIS						NOUGHT
		28						GOD
	NOUGHT	7:	THERE	WIS	IS	FOR	LOVES	28

"FOR THERE IS NOUGHT GOD LOVES,
be it not one who dwells with Wisdom."
WIS 7: 28

	WIS	FAIRER		FOR			SHE	
THE					THAN			IS
					FAIRER			7:29
	SHE	THAN		SUN				
WIS								THAN
				7:29		FAIRER	THE	
FAIRER			IS					
SUN			WIS					THE
	FOR			SHE		WIS	THAN	

"FOR SHE IS FAIRER THAN THE SUN and surpasses
every constellation of the stars."
WIS 7:29

PUZZLE **46**

	DID		WIS		8		AVAIL	
US			5:	PRIDE	AVAIL			OUR
		WHAT				8		
DID	8						OUR	WIS
	WHAT			AVAIL			PRIDE	
5:	PRIDE						8	WHAT
		WIS				OUR		
WHAT			US	8	WIS			AVAIL
	AVAIL		WHAT		DID		US	

"WHAT DID OUR PRIDE AVAIL US?
What have wealth and its boastfulness afforded us?"
WIS 5: 8

		NOW	CHILD	WAS	A	I		
	WELL						FAVORED	
	8:19							
	I	A						
		CHILD	A	WELL	I	WAS		
						A	NOW	
							A	
	FAVORED						8:19	
		WELL	8:19	FAVORED	CHILD	NOW		

"NOW, I WAS A <u>WELL</u>-<u>FAVORED</u> CHILD,
and I came by a noble nature."
WIS <u>8:19</u>

PUZZLE **48**

		YOUR				ME		
			THRONE	GIVE	ME			
AT			WIS 9:4		THE			THRONE
	ATTENDANT	WIS 9:4				GIVE	ME	
	THE						THRONE	
	GIVE	AT				THE	WISDOM	
ME			GIVE		WISDOM			YOUR
			ATTENDANT	WIS 9:4	AT			
		THRONE				WIS 9:4		

"GIVE ME WISDOM, THE ATTENDANT AT YOUR THRONE,
and reject me not from among your children."
WIS 9:4

IN	KEEL			ITS			NO	OF
THE								WIS 5:10
			NO	IN	PATH			
		OF	KEEL		THE	WIS 5:10		
NO		ITS				WAVES		THE
	IN	ITS		WAVES	NO			
			WIS 5:10	THE	IN			
WIS 5:10								WAVES
OF	NO			WAVES			WIS 5:10	IN

"Like a ship traversing the heaving water, of which,
when it has passed, no trace can be found,
NO PATH OF ITS KEEL IN THE WAVES."
WIS 5:10

PUZZLE **50**

	HE						WIS	
HER			WATCHES		WHO			HE
		DAWN		AT		6:14		
	FOR			WHO			HER	
		WHO	HE		FOR	WATCHES		
	HER			DAWN			AT	
		HER		HE		WIS		
WIS			WHO		AT			HER
	WHO						DAWN	

"HE WHO WATCHES FOR HER AT DAWN shall not be disappointed, for he shall find her sitting by his gate."
<u>WIS 6:14</u>

KNOWS			WIS		FOR			9:11
	THINGS						FOR	
		UNDER-STANDS				KNOWS		
UNDER-STANDS				KNOWS				FOR
			SHE	9:11	WIS			
SHE				UNDER-STANDS				ALL
		AND				THINGS		
	FOR						UNDER-STANDS	
ALL			9:11		UNDER-STANDS			SHE

"FOR SHE KNOWS AND UNDERSTANDS ALL THINGS,
and will guide me discreetly in my affairs and
safeguard me by her glory."
WIS 9:11

PUZZLE **52**

			`				JUST	ABANDON
	SHE	DID	10:13	JUST				THE
	10:13		NOT					
	ABANDON	MAN						
	JUST			10:13			NOT	
						WIS	10:13	
					MAN		WIS	
NOT				ABANDON	DID	THE	SHE	
SHE	DID							

"SHE DID NOT ABANDON THE JUST MAN
when he was sold, but delivered him from sin."
<u>WIS 10:13</u>

	OF					A		
FOLLY	LEFT			MEMORIAL		MANKIND	OF	
			FOLLY		THEY			
		THEIR				OF		
	FOLLY						MEMORIAL	
		A				WIS 10:8		
			THEIR	WIS 10:8				
OF	MANKIND			A			FOLLY	THEIR
	THEY						LEFT	

"For those who forsook Wisdom first were bereft of knowledge of the right, and then THEY LEFT MANKIND A MEMORIAL OF THEIR FOLLY—so that they could not even be hidden in their fall."
<u>WIS 10:8</u>

PUZZLE **54**

	THEIR	FOR	RETURN	THOUGHTS		IN	SENSELESS	
WIS 11:15				SENSELESS				FOR
SENSELESS				IN				RETURN
	WICKED	WIS 11:15						SENSELESS
FOR			WIS 11:15	RETURN				WICKED
IN						AND	WIS 11:15	
THOUGHTS			THEIR					WIS 11:15
THEIR			FOR					IN
	WIS 11:15	AND		SENSELESS	THOUGHTS	FOR	WICKED	

"AND IN RETURN FOR THEIR SENSELESS,
WICKED THOUGHTS, which misled them into worshiping dumb
serpents and worthless insects, You sent upon them swarms of
dumb creatures for vengeance."
<u>WIS 11:15</u>

			PRODUCTS	NOT IDLE	BE			
	OF YOUR	PRODUCTS	YOU WILL		THAT	NOT IDLE	THE	
	BE						PRODUCTS	
YOU WILL	WIS 14:5			OF YOUR			THAT	WISDOM
THAT			THE		WISDOM			WIS 14:5
WISDOM	PRODUCTS			YOU WILL			BE	NOT IDLE
	THE						NOT IDLE	
	YOU WILL	NOT IDLE	WIS 14:5		PRODUCTS	OF YOUR	WISDOM	
			NOT IDLE	THAT	OF YOUR			

"But <u>YOU WILL</u> THAT THE PRODUCTS <u>OF YOUR</u> WISDOM BE <u>NOT IDLE</u>; therefore men trust their lives even to frailest wood, and have been safe crossing the surge on a raft."
<u>WIS 14:5</u>

PUZZLE **56**

	ALWAYS			11:21			ABIDES	
YOU	STRENGTH						FOR	GREAT
		WIS	FOR	STRENGTH	ABIDES	WITH		
		GREAT				ALWAYS		
WITH		YOU				GREAT		ABIDES
		11:21				YOU		
		STRENGTH	YOU	FOR	WIS	ABIDES		
ABIDES	GREAT						YOU	11:21
	YOU			GREAT			STRENGTH	

"FOR WITH YOU GREAT STRENGTH ABIDES ALWAYS;
who can resist the might of your arm?"
WIS 11:21

HOW	POWERFUL						MORE	MUCH
MADE								WIS 13:4
			IS HE		THEM			
		THEM			MUCH	IS HE		
		WHO		MORE		HOW		
		MADE	HOW			POWERFUL		
			WIS 13:4		POWERFUL			
WHO								THEM
MORE	IS HE						WHO	POWERFUL

"Or if they were struck by their might and energy,
let them from these things realize HOW MUCH
MORE POWERFUL IS HE WHO MADE THEM."
WIS 13:4

	WERE			THESE			12:8	
			WIS		EVEN			
		WIS	12:8		MEN	WERE		
	BUT	THEY				EVEN	WIS	
THESE								BUT
	12:8	AS				MEN	WERE	
		WERE	THEY		THESE	AS		
			BUT		AS			
	EVEN			MEN			THESE	

"BUT EVEN THESE, AS THEY WERE MEN, you spared,
and sent wasps as forerunners of your army that
they might exterminate them by degrees."
WIS 12:8

WIS 15:1				ARE				
GOOD			BUT		AND			
TRUE			GOOD		YOU			
		YOU				GOD		
	WIS 15:1			TRUE			YOU	
		ARE				GOOD		
			OUR		WIS 15:1			ARE
			ARE		GOD			OUR
				YOU				BUT

"BUT YOU, OUR GOD, ARE GOOD AND TRUE,
slow to anger, and governing all with mercy."
WIS 15:1

PUZZLE **60**

14:13				THEY				FOR
			FOR		THE			
		WERE				IN		
	THE		IN		NOT		THEY	
	FOR						NOT	
	14:13		THE		FOR		BEGINNING	
		IN				WIS		
			WERE		IN			
BEGINNING				FOR				THEY

"FOR IN THE BEGINNING THEY WERE NOT,
nor shall they continue forever."
WIS 14:13

			YOUR	WIS	ESCAPE			
BUT	YOUR						15	CAN
WIS	16:						BUT	HAND
			WIS	BUT	16:			
ESCAPE	CAN						16:	YOUR
CAN	HAND						ESCAPE	16:
			16:	15	NONE			

"BUT YOUR HAND NONE CAN ESCAPE."
WIS <u>16</u>: <u>15</u>

PUZZLE **62**

BUT		HAD				WIS 18:1		YOUR
		VERY				LIGHT		
WIS 18:1	HOLY		ONES		LIGHT		HAD	VERY
		GREAT		ONES		BUT		
			HOLY	VERY	GREAT			
		LIGHT		YOUR		VERY		
LIGHT	GREAT		YOUR		WIS 18:1		VERY	BUT
		HOLY				YOUR		
VERY		BUT				HOLY		LIGHT

"BUT YOUR HOLY ONES HAD VERY GREAT LIGHT; and these others, who heard their voices but did not see their forms, since now they themselves had suffered, called them blest."
<u>WIS 18:1</u>

			YET	BEFORE-HAND	FOR HE			
		FOR HE				KNEW		
	WHAT			WIS 19:1			WERE	
	THEY					WHAT		
		WERE	YET	BEFORE-HAND				
	YET					TO DO		
	WIS 19:1			KNEW			YET	
	KNEW					BEFORE-HAND		
			WHAT	WERE	TO DO			

"But the wicked, merciless wrath assailed until the end.
FOR HE KNEW BEFOREHAND WHAT
THEY WERE YET TO DO."
WIS 19:1

PUZZLE **64**

SIR 28:26				SLIP				TAKE
			TAKE		NOT			
		BY				CARE		
	NOT		CARE		YOUR		SLIP	
	TAKE						YOUR	
	SIR 28:26		NOT		TAKE		TO	
		CARE				TONGUE		
			BY		CARE			
TO				TAKE				SLIP

"TAKE CARE NOT TO SLIP BY YOUR TONGUE
and fall victim to your foe waiting in ambush."
<u>SIR 28:26</u>

ALL	LORD	WISDOM	SIR	1	FROM	COMES	THE	1:
SIR	THE						ALL	FROM
COMES				THE				WISDOM
LORD				WISDOM				SIR
THE		SIR	COMES	FROM	1	ALL		LORD
1				ALL				THE
1:				COMES				ALL
WISDOM	1			1:			SIR	COMES
FROM	ALL	COMES	THE	SIR	LORD	1:	WISDOM	1

"ALL WISDOM COMES FROM THE LORD
and with him it remains forever."
SIR 1: 1

PUZZLE **66**

	MY SON	TO	YOU					
	THE		SERVE			TO	YOU	COME
	COME	SIR 2:1	THE			MY SON		LORD
						SERVE	MY SON	THE
				LORD				
WHEN	YOU	COME						
THE		MY SON			YOU	SIR 2:1	LORD	
COME	LORD	SERVE			TO		WHEN	
					THE	COME	TO	

"<u>MY SON</u>, WHEN YOU COME TO SERVE THE LORD,
prepare yourself for trials."
<u>SIR 2:1</u>

		AVERT	FROM	COMELY	9:8	EYES		
	WOMAN			SIR			AVERT	
	COMELY						9:8	
			A					
EYES		YOUR				FROM		SIR
			FROM					
	AVERT						A	
	9:8		AVERT				WOMAN	
		COMELY	A	YOUR	WOMAN	9:8		

"AVERT YOUR EYES FROM A COMELY WOMAN;
gaze not upon the beauty of another's wife."
SIR 9:8

	SIR	PRIDE						SIN
SIN			RESERVOIR					
OF			IS			FOR		
	FOR	10:13			PRIDE			
				IS				
			THE			SIR	IS	
		OF			IS			PRIDE
					FOR			RESERVOIR
PRIDE						OF	SIN	

"FOR PRIDE IS THE RESERVOIR OF SIN, a source which runs over with vice; because of it God sends unheard-of afflictions and brings men to utter ruin."
SIR 10:13

PUZZLE **69**

					HE		FATHER	
HONORS	LORD	THE			SIR 3:7		HE	
					WHO		HONORS	
WHO	HONORS	SIR 3:7						
						HONORS	LORD	SIR 3:7
	FATHER		THE					
	THE		FATHER			LORD	WHO	FEARS
	FEARS		HIS					

"HE WHO FEARS THE LORD HONORS HIS FATHER,
and serves his parents as rulers."
SIR 3:7

		NOT	7:8	DO	REPEAT	PLOT		
	PLOT						A	
REPEAT								
A								
TO				SIR	DO	REPEAT	7:8	SIN
SIN								NOT
PLOT								7:8
	DO						TO	
		SIR	PLOT	REPEAT	NOT	SIN		

"DO NOT PLOT TO REPEAT A SIN;
not even for one will you go unpunished."
<u>SIR</u> <u>7:8</u>

IF YOU		WISH				YOU		BE
			YOU	CAN	BE			
	TAUGHT	MY	BE		IF YOU	WISH	CAN	
WISH				MY				SON
	SON	SIR 6:32	CAN		YOU	IF YOU	TAUGHT	
			WISH	IF YOU	SON			
SON		BE				TAUGHT		CAN

"MY SON, <u>IF YOU</u> WISH, YOU CAN BE TAUGHT;
if you apply yourself, you will be shrewd."
<u>SIR 6:32</u>

THOSE	LORD						THE	LOVES
WHO		SIR				HER		4:14
HER			WHO	4:14	THOSE			SIR
	THE						LORD	
LOVES			LOVE		4:14			THE
LORD		LOVE						HER
SIR			4:14	LOVE	THE			THOSE
	THOSE						4:14	
		WHO	SIR	THOSE	LOVES	THE		

"Those who serve her serve the Holy One;
THOSE WHO LOVE HER THE LORD LOVES."
SIR 4:14

					HE	WILL	WHO	
WHO	DANGER	WILL	IT				LOVES	
HE			WHO				IN	
DANGER				HE		IT	SIR 3:25	
	PERISH	WHO		SIR 3:25				DANGER
	WHO				PERISH			LOVES
	LOVES				SIR 3:25	IN	WILL	WHO
	WILL	SIR 3:25	DANGER					

"A stubborn man will fare badly in the end, and
HE WHO LOVES DANGER WILL PERISH IN IT."
SIR 3:25

							BUT	SWIFT
	SLOW	TO	5:13				SIR	BE
	TO HEAR		SLOW					
	5:13	SIR	SWIFT					
					BE	TO	TO HEAR	
					ANSWER		BE	
SWIFT	BE				BUT	5:13	ANSWER	
5:13	ANSWER							

"BE SWIFT <u>TO HEAR,</u> BUT SLOW TO ANSWER."
<u>SIR</u> <u>5:13</u>

A								BITTEN
	HE IS	WHEN	WHO				PITIES	
				PITIES			CHARMER	
					SNAKE	WHEN	BITTEN	
	PITIES	WHO	A					
	SIR 12:13			SNAKE				
	WHEN				SIR 12:13	HE IS	A	
SNAKE								SIR 12:13

'WHO PITIES A SNAKE CHARMER WHEN <u>HE IS</u> BITTEN,
or anyone who goes near a wild beast?"
<u>SIR 12:13</u>

		YOUR			SIR	EVERY	HOUSE	
				INTO				11:29
		EVERY		NOT				YOUR
		HOUSE					SIR	
		INTO				MAN		
	11:29					BRING		
SIR				11:29		YOUR		
NOT				EVERY				
	YOUR	MAN	SIR			HOUSE		

"BRING NOT EVERY MAN INTO YOUR HOUSE, for many are the snares of the crafty one."
SIR 11:29

	EVER	IS				SIR	13:16	
SIR			EVER		IS			WITH
ALLIED			WITH		13:16			EVER
A WOLF			A		LAMB			13:16
	SIR	WITH	IS			ALLIED	EVER	A
			SIR					A WOLF
			LAMB					SIR
A			A WOLF		SIR			ALLIED
	LAMB	SIR				WITH	A WOLF	

"IS <u>A WOLF</u> EVER ALLIED WITH A LAMB?
So it is with the sinner and the just."
<u>SIR 13:16</u>

				LORD				
		HE		WHO				
		SIR 15:1				THIS		
		THIS		HE		WILL		
	WILL	LORD				THE	THIS	
FEARS	THE	WHO		THIS		HE	LORD	DO
		WILL				DO		
	WHO	THE	FEARS		WILL	SIR 15:1	HE	
LORD	DO			SIR 15:1			WHO	WILL

"HE WHO FEARS THE LORD WILL DO THIS;
he who is practiced in the law will come to wisdom."
SIR 15:1

			DOES	SIR	REWARD			
		REWARD				DOES		
	16:		HAS		HIS		SIR	
14		WHOEVER				REWARD		HIS
16:				REWARD				GOOD
SIR		HAS				14		16:
	14		16:		HAS		REWARD	
		DOES				HIS		
			HIS	GOOD	SIR			

"WHOEVER DOES GOOD HAS HIS REWARD,
which each receives according to his deeds."
SIR 16: 14

PUZZLE **80**

					BRINGS	NO	HIM	
				WHOSE				
	SIR 14:1	MAN	HIM		NO	WHOSE	THE	
SIR 14:1	WHOSE			BRINGS			MOUTH	THE
NO								HIM
MOUTH								NO
GRIEF								WHOSE
	MOUTH						MAN	
		WHOSE	GRIEF	NO	SIR 14:1	HIM		

"Happy THE MAN WHOSE MOUTH BRINGS HIM
NO GRIEF, who is not stung by remorse for sin."
SIR 14:1

	PATIENT	IS WHY	WITH	SIR 18:9	LORD			
		MEN			THE	SIR 18:9	THAT	
		SIR 18:9			MEN			IS WHY
	THE					LORD		WITH
IS							MEN	PATIENT
SIR 18:9							THE	
	WITH					PATIENT		
		PATIENT			THAT			
			IS	WITH				

"THAT IS WHY THE LORD IS PATIENT WITH MEN
and showers upon them his mercy."
SIR 18:9

	SIR 17:20	AND	UP			RETURN		
	TO			THE	GIVE		SIR 17:20	AND
SIN					SIR 17:20			TO
	LORD	SIN						UP
	UP			AND			LORD	
AND						SIR 17:20	SIN	
LORD			TO					GIVE
THE	RETURN		GIVE	LORD			AND	
		GIVE			RETURN	TO	UP	

"RETURN TO THE LORD AND GIVE UP SIN,
pray to him and make your offenses few."
SIR 17:20

BLANDISH-MENTS	VAIN				POUR			
POUR			20:12			VAIN	THEIR	
			BLANDISH-MENTS	FOOLS			SIR	
	20:12	POUR	FORTH					VAIN
		THEIR		IN		SIR		
VAIN					FOOLS	20:12	FORTH	
	THEIR			FORTH	IN			
	POUR	BLANDISH-MENTS			SIR			FORTH
			THEIR				POUR	20:12

"A wise man makes himself popular by a few words, but FOOLS POUR FORTH THEIR BLANDISHMENTS IN VAIN."
SIR 20:12

PUZZLE **84**

			IN	RAISES	A			
		LAUGHTER			FOOL			
	HIS			VOICE				
SIR				A				
21:20				FOOL			SIR	RAISES
FOOL					IN	HIS		VOICE
	IN							FOOL
		SIR					VOICE	
			HIS	SIR	LAUGHTER	21:20		

"A FOOL RAISES HIS VOICE IN LAUGHTER,
but the prudent man at the most smiles gently."
SIR 21:20

OVER	WHO							
		SET	GUARD					
				SET	SIR 22:27	MOUTH		
		MY	WHO					
WILL	A						OVER	GUARD
					OVER	WILL		
		GUARD	OVER	MY				
					WILL	WHO		
							A	SET

"WHO WILL SET A GUARD OVER MY MOUTH,
and upon my lips an effective seal, that I may not fail
through them, that my tongue may not destroy me?"
SIR 22:27

PUZZLE **86**

						OF	WISDOM	
					19:17	IS	THE	LORD
				WISDOM	FEAR	19:17		ALL
			IS	LORD		FEAR	19:17	THE
		FEAR	WISDOM					
THE	LORD	ALL						
FEAR		19:17	ALL					
LORD			THE					
WISDOM	SIR	IS	19:17					

"ALL WISDOM IS FEAR OF THE LORD; perfect wisdom
is the fulfillment of the law."
SIR 19:17

SIR	26:							
IS A	GOOD				WIFE	SIR	A	
					GIFT		3	
					3	A	GIFT	
	WIFE	IS A	GOOD					
	GENEROUS		IS A					
	3	26:	SIR				GENEROUS	WIFE
							SIR	3

"A GOOD WIFE <u>IS A</u> GENEROUS GIFT
bestowed upon him who fears the LORD."
<u>SIR</u> <u>26</u>: <u>3</u>

TWO		MEN	23:					SINS
		16	SIR					
			16				SIR	TYPES
						MEN	SINS	16
				OF				
SIR	23:	MULTIPLY						
16	TYPES				TWO			
					23:	SINS		
23:					MULTIPLY	TWO		OF

"TWO TYPES OF MEN MULTIPLY SINS, a third draws down wrath; for burning passion is a blazing fire, not to be quenched till it burns itself out: a man given to sins of the flesh, who never stops until the fire breaks forth."
SIR 23: 16

IN				YOU				
	WHAT		IN		NOT			
		SAVED				YOUR		
	YOUR		SAVED				HAVE	
SIR 25:3				HAVE				YOU
	YOUTH				IN		SIR 25:3	
		YOU				SAVED		
			YOU		WHAT		IN	
				YOUTH				WHAT

"WHAT YOU HAVE NOT SAVED IN YOUR YOUTH,
how will you acquire in your old age?"
SIR 25:3

PUZZLE **90**

		WILL		FEWER		SIR 28:8		
	BE		AND		SIR 28:8		STRIFE	
	SINS						YOUR	
		SIR 28:8	AVOID	AND	BE	WILL		
			SIR 28:8		WILL			
			FEWER		SINS			
	SIR 28:8	FEWER				BE	AND	
STRIFE								FEWER
	YOUR	AND	STRIFE	BE	FEWER	SINS	AVOID	

"AVOID STRIFE AND YOUR SINS WILL BE FEWER,
for a quarrelsome man kindles disputes."
SIR 28:8

						WHO		
	THE	FEARS			WHO		LORD	
	SIR 33:1			LORD		THE MAN		CAN
					THE		FEARS	
		HARM				NO EVIL		
	LORD		WHO					
NO EVIL		SIR 33:1		FEARS			THE MAN	
	WHO		HARM			LORD	SIR 33:1	
		CAN						

"NO EVIL CAN HARM THE MAN WHO FEARS THE LORD;
through trials, again and again he is safe."
SIR 33:1

PUZZLE 92

1

TOB	AND	YOUR	3:2	ALL	MERCY	WAYS	TRUTH	ARE
ALL	WAYS	ARE	TOB	YOUR	TRUTH	3:2	AND	MERCY
MERCY	3:2	TRUTH	ARE	WAYS	AND	ALL	YOUR	TOB
AND	MERCY	3:2	YOUR	TRUTH	WAYS	ARE	TOB	ALL
ARE	YOUR	WAYS	AND	TOB	ALL	MERCY	3:2	TRUTH
TRUTH	TOB	ALL	MERCY	3:2	ARE	AND	WAYS	YOUR
WAYS	TRUTH	AND	ALL	ARE	TOB	YOUR	MERCY	3:2
YOUR	ALL	MERCY	TRUTH	AND	3:2	TOB	ARE	WAYS
3:2	ARE	TOB	WAYS	MERCY	YOUR	TRUTH	ALL	AND

2

MAY	MINDFUL	YOU	LORD	ME	O	BE	TOB 3:3	OF
ME	TOB 3:3	LORD	BE	MINDFUL	OF	O	YOU	MAY
O	OF	BE	MAY	TOB 3:3	YOU	MINDFUL	LORD	ME
BE	ME	O	OF	LORD	MAY	YOU	MINDFUL	TOB 3:3
YOU	MAY	MINDFUL	TOB 3:3	O	ME	OF	BE	LORD
OF	LORD	TOB 3:3	MINDFUL	YOU	BE	MAY	ME	O
TOB 3:3	BE	MAY	ME	OF	MINDFUL	LORD	O	YOU
MINDFUL	O	ME	YOU	MAY	LORD	TOB 3:3	OF	BE
LORD	YOU	OF	O	BE	TOB 3:3	ME	MAY	MINDFUL

3

YES	AND	3:5	ARE	TOB	JUDG-MENTS	YOUR	MANY	TRUE
YOUR	JUDG-MENTS	TOB	MANY	TRUE	AND	ARE	YES	3:5
ARE	TRUE	MANY	YOUR	3:5	YES	AND	JUDG-MENTS	TOB
3:5	MANY	YES	TRUE	ARE	TOB	JUDG-MENTS	AND	YOUR
TRUE	YOUR	ARE	JUDG-MENTS	AND	3:5	YES	TOB	MANY
AND	TOB	JUDG-MENTS	YES	MANY	YOUR	3:5	TRUE	ARE
TOB	ARE	AND	3:5	JUDG-MENT	MANY	TRUE	YOUR	YES
MANY	YES	TRUE	AND	YOUR	ARE	TOB	3:5	JUDG-MENTS
JUDG-MENTS	3:5	YOUR	TOB	YES	TRUE	MANY	ARE	AND

4

BLESSED	TOB	3:11	GOD	YOU	MERCIFUL	LORD	O	ARE
GOD	LORD	MERCIFUL	3:11	O	ARE	YOU	TOB	BLESSED
O	YOU	ARE	LORD	BLESSED	TOB	GOD	3:11	MERCIFUL
MERCIFUL	3:11	TOB	ARE	GOD	YOU	BLESSED	LORD	O
YOU	O	BLESSED	MERCIFUL	LORD	3:11	TOB	ARE	GOD
LORD	ARE	GOD	O	TOB	BLESSED	MERCIFUL	YOU	3:11
TOB	MERCIFUL	O	YOU	3:11	GOD	ARE	BLESSED	LORD
ARE	BLESSED	LORD	TOB	MERCIFUL	O	3:11	GOD	YOU
3:11	GOD	YOU	BLESSED	ARE	LORD	O	MERCIFUL	TOB

5

O LORD	FACE	MY	TOB 3:12	TO YOU	AND	I	NOW	TURN
NOW	TO YOU	I	FACE	TURN	MY	AND	O LORD	TOB 3:12
AND	TOB 3:12	TURN	NOW	O LORD	I	TO YOU	MY	FACE
TO YOU	MY	O LORD	TURN	AND	NOW	FACE	TOB 3:12	I
TOB 3:12	AND	FACE	O LORD	I	TO YOU	NOW	TURN	MY
I	TURN	NOW	MY	TOB 3:12	FACE	O LORD	AND	TO YOU
FACE	NOW	AND	I	MY	TURN	TOB 3:12	TO YOU	O LORD
TURN	O LORD	TO YOU	AND	FACE	TOB 3:12	MY	I	NOW
MY	I	TOB 3:12	TO YOU	NOW	O LORD	TURN	FACE	AND

6

THAT	KNOW	I	TOB 3:14	MASTER	INNOCENT	O	AM	YOU
AM	YOU	INNOCENT	O	THAT	I	KNOW	MASTER	TOB 3:14
TOB 3:14	MASTER	O	AM	KNOW	YOU	INNOCENT	THAT	I
YOU	O	AM	MASTER	I	KNOW	TOB 3:14	INNOCENT	THAT
I	INNOCENT	THAT	YOU	AM	TOB 3:14	MASTER	KNOW	O
MASTER	TOB 3:14	KNOW	THAT	INNOCENT	O	YOU	I	AM
INNOCENT	THAT	YOU	KNOW	TOB 3:14	AM	I	O	MASTER
KNOW	AM	TOB 3:14	I	O	MASTER	THAT	YOU	INNOCENT
O	I	MASTER	INNOCENT	YOU	THAT	AM	TOB 3:14	KNOW

7

THE	GIVE	TO	HUNGRY	OF	SOME	TOB 4:16	YOUR	BREAD
SOME	YOUR	OF	GIVE	TOB 4:16	BREAD	HUNGRY	TO	THE
BREAD	HUNGRY	TOB 4:16	YOUR	TO	THE	GIVE	SOME	OF
YOUR	THE	SOME	TOB 4:16	GIVE	HUNGRY	OF	BREAD	TO
OF	BREAD	HUNGRY	SOME	YOUR	TO	THE	TOB 4:16	GIVE
TOB 4:16	TO	GIVE	THE	BREAD	OF	SOME	HUNGRY	YOUR
TO	TOB 4:16	THE	OF	HUNGRY	YOUR	BREAD	GIVE	SOME
GIVE	OF	BREAD	TO	SOME	TOB 4:16	YOUR	THE	HUNGRY
HUNGRY	SOME	YOUR	BREAD	THE	GIVE	TO	OF	TOB 4:16

8

EXALT	13:7	FOR	ME	I	TOB	AS	MY	GOD
TOB	ME	GOD	FOR	AS	MY	13:7	I	EXALT
AS	MY	I	GOD	EXALT	13:7	FOR	ME	TOB
GOD	I	ME	AS	TOB	EXALT	MY	13:7	FOR
13:7	FOR	TOB	I	MY	GOD	EXALT	AS	ME
MY	AS	EXALT	13:7	FOR	ME	GOD	TOB	I
FOR	GOD	AS	MY	ME	I	TOB	EXALT	13:7
I	TOB	MY	EXALT	13.7	FOR	ME	GOD	AS
ME	EXALT	13:7	TOB	GOD	AS	I	FOR	MY

9

HAS	GOD	BLESSED	WHO	BE	RAISED	UP	TOB 13:18	YOU
UP	TOB 13:18	BE	GOD	YOU	BLESSED	RAISED	WHO	HAS
WHO	RAISED	YOU	HAS	UP	TOB 13:18	BE	BLESSED	GOD
BE	WHO	GOD	RAISED	HAS	YOU	BLESSED	UP	TOB 13:18
YOU	UP	HAS	BLESSED	TOB 13:18	BE	WHO	GOD	RAISED
TOB 13:18	BLESSED	RAISED	UP	WHO	GOD	YOU	HAS	BE
BLESSED	BE	WHO	YOU	GOD	HAS	TOB 13:18	RAISED	UP
RAISED	HAS	TOB 13:18	BE	BLESSED	UP	GOD	YOU	WHO
GOD	YOU	UP	TOB 13:18	RAISED	WHO	HAS	BE	BLESSED

10

SONG	SING	HIM	1	NEW	16:	TO	JDT	A
A	16:	JDT	SING	SONG	TO	NEW	1	HIM
TO	NEW	1	JDT	A	HIM	16:	SONG	SING
JDT	1	16:	A	SING	NEW	SONG	HIM	TO
SING	SONG	NEW	TO	HIM	JDT	A	16:	1
HIM	A	TO	SONG	16:	1	SING	NEW	JDT
1	HIM	SONG	NEW	TO	SING	JDT	A	16:
16:	TO	A	HIM	JDT	SONG	1	SING	NEW
NEW	JDT	SING	16:	1	A	HIM	TO	SONG

11

WILL	JDT 16:13	MY	A NEW	I	HYMN	TO	GOD	SING
SING	HYMN	TO	WILL	MY	GOD	I	JDT 16:13	A NEW
GOD	I	A NEW	JDT 16:13	TO	SING	MY	WILL	HYMN
I	A NEW	GOD	MY	HYMN	TO	JDT 16:13	SING	WILL
MY	TO	SING	GOD	WILL	JDT 16:13	A NEW	HYMN	I
JDT 16:13	WILL	HYMN	I	SING	A NEW	GOD	MY	TO
A NEW	MY	WILL	SING	JDT 16:13	I	HYMN	TO	GOD
HYMN	GOD	JDT 16:13	TO	A NEW	WILL	SING	I	MY
TO	SING	I	HYMN	GOD	MY	WILL	A NEW	JDT 16:13

12

SAMARIA	ALL	AND	JDT 1:9	IN	CITIES	THOSE	ITS	TO
ITS	TO	CITIES	THOSE	SAMARIA	AND	ALL	IN	JDT 1:9
JDT 1:9	IN	THOSE	ITS	ALL	TO	CITIES	SAMARIA	AND
TO	THOSE	ITS	IN	AND	ALL	JDT 1:9	CITIES	SAMARIA
AND	CITIES	SAMARIA	TO	ITS	JDT 1:9	IN	ALL	THOSE
IN	JDT 1:9	ALL	SAMARIA	CITIES	THOSE	TO	AND	ITS
CITIES	SAMARIA	TO	ALL	JDT 1:9	ITS	AND	THOSE	IN
ALL	ITS	JDT 1:9	AND	THOSE	IN	SAMARIA	TO	CITIES
THOSE	AND	IN	CITIES	TO	SAMARIA	ITS	JDT 1:9	ALL

13

EARTH	READY	TO	THEM	AND	TELL	HAVE	WATER	JDT 2:7
THEM	AND	HAVE	READY	JDT 2:7	WATER	TELL	TO	EARTH
JDT 2:7	WATER	TELL	TO	HAVE	EARTH	READY	THEM	AND
TELL	JDT 2:7	AND	EARTH	READY	TO	WATER	HAVE	THEM
HAVE	TO	THEM	WATER	TELL	JDT 2:7	EARTH	AND	READY
READY	EARTH	WATER	AND	THEM	HAVE	JDT 2:7	TELL	TO
TO	TELL	READY	HAVE	EARTH	AND	THEM	JDT 2:7	WATER
AND	THEM	JDT 2:7	TELL	WATER	READY	TO	EARTH	HAVE
WATER	HAVE	EARTH	JDT 2:7	TO	THEM	AND	READY	TELL

14

FOR	QUARTER	JDT 2:11	NO	WHO	THEM	SHOW	RESIST	THOSE
NO	SHOW	THEM	JDT 2:11	RESIST	THOSE	WHO	QUARTER	FOR
RESIST	WHO	THOSE	SHOW	FOR	QUARTER	NO	JDT 2:11	THEM
THEM	JDT 2:11	QUARTER	THOSE	NO	WHO	FOR	SHOW	RESIST
WHO	RESIST	FOR	THEM	SHOW	JDT 2:11	QUARTER	THOSE	NO
SHOW	THOSE	NO	RESIST	QUARTER	FOR	THEM	WHO	JDT 2:11
QUARTER	THEM	RESIST	WHO	JDT 2:11	NO	THOSE	FOR	SHOW
THOSE	FOR	SHOW	QUARTER	THEM	RESIST	JDT 2:11	NO	WHO
JDT 2:11	NO	WHO	FOR	THOSE	SHOW	RESIST	THEM	QUARTER

15

OR	JDT	EARTH	2:20	THE	LIKE	DUST	LOCUSTS	OF THE
LOCUSTS	THE	DUST	JDT	OF THE	EARTH	LIKE	OR	2:20
LIKE	2:20	OF THE	LOCUSTS	OR	DUST	THE	EARTH	JDT
THE	EARTH	OR	OF THE	LIKE	LOCUSTS	JDT	2:20	DUST
2:20	LIKE	JDT	OR	DUST	THE	LOCUSTS	OF THE	EARTH
DUST	OF THE	LOCUSTS	EARTH	2:20	JDT	OR	LIKE	THE
JDT	LOCUSTS	LIKE	DUST	EARTH	OF THE	2:20	THE	OR
OF THE	OR	THE	LIKE	JDT	2:20	EARTH	DUST	LOCUSTS
EARTH	DUST	2:20	THE	LOCUSTS	OR	OF THE	JDT	LIKE

16

ALL	AND	PUT	THEIR	TO	YOUTHS	JDT 2:27	THE	SWORD
YOUTHS	THE	TO	AND	JDT 2:27	SWORD	THEIR	PUT	ALL
SWORD	THEIR	JDT 2:27	THE	PUT	ALL	AND	YOUTHS	TO
THE	ALL	YOUTHS	JDT 2:27	AND	THEIR	TO	SWORD	PUT
TO	SWORD	THEIR	YOUTHS	THE	PUT	ALL	JDT 2:27	AND
JDT 2:27	PUT	AND	ALL	SWORD	TO	YOUTHS	THEIR	THE
PUT	JDT 2:27	ALL	TO	THEIR	THE	SWORD	AND	YOUTHS
AND	TO	SWORD	PUT	YOUTHS	JDT 2:27	THE	ALL	THEIR
THEIR	YOUTHS	THE	SWORD	ALL	AND	PUT	TO	JDT 2:27

17

FELL	THE	AND	JDT 2:28	OF HIM	ALL	FEAR	UPON	DREAD
DREAD	ALL	UPON	THE	FELL	FEAR	OF HIM	JDT 2:28	AND
FEAR	OF HIM	JDT 2:28	UPON	DREAD	AND	ALL	FELL	THE
UPON	JDT 2:28	ALL	DREAD	THE	OF HIM	FELL	AND	FEAR
THE	FELL	OF HIM	FEAR	AND	UPON	DREAD	ALL	JDT 2:28
AND	DREAD	FEAR	FELL	ALL	JDT 2:28	THE	OF HIM	UPON
JDT 2:28	AND	FELL	OF HIM	FEAR	THE	UPON	DREAD	ALL
ALL	FEAR	DREAD	AND	UPON	FELL	JDT 2:28	THE	OF HIM
OF HIM	UPON	THE	ALL	JDT 2:28	DREAD	AND	FEAR	FELL

18

MAKE	AS	3:3	USE	PLEASE	YOU	JDT	OF	THEM
THEM	PLEASE	YOU	MAKE	JDT	OF	USE	AS	3:3
USE	JDT	OF	THEM	3:3	AS	MAKE	PLEASE	YOU
3:3	OF	MAKE	PLEASE	THEM	JDT	YOU	USE	AS
JDT	USE	AS	3:3	YOU	MAKE	PLEASE	THEM	OF
PLEASE	YOU	THEM	OF	AS	USE	3:3	MAKE	JDT
AS	3:3	PLEASE	JDT	USE	THEM	OF	YOU	MAKE
OF	THEM	USE	YOU	MAKE	3:3	AS	JDT	PLEASE
YOU	MAKE	JDT	AS	OF	PLEASE	THEM	3:3	USE

19

WITH	JDT 3:4	SEE	COME	DEAL	AND	AS YOU	FIT	THEM
THEM	AND	AS YOU	WITH	SEE	FIT	DEAL	JDT 3:4	COME
FIT	DEAL	COME	JDT 3:4	AS YOU	THEM	SEE	WITH	AND
DEAL	COME	FIT	SEE	AND	AS YOU	JDT 3:4	THEM	WITH
SEE	AS YOU	THEM	FIT	WITH	JDT 3:4	COME	AND	DEAL
JDT 3:4	WITH	AND	DEAL	THEM	COME	FIT	SEE	AS YOU
COME	SEE	WITH	THEM	JDT 3:4	DEAL	AND	AS YOU	FIT
AND	FIT	JDT 3:4	AS YOU	COME	WITH	THEM	DEAL	SEE
AS YOU	THEM	DEAL	AND	FIT	SEE	WITH	COME	JDT 3:4

20

WITH	JDT	HIS	6	WENT	3:	ARMY	DOWN	HE
DOWN	ARMY	6	HIS	HE	JDT	3:	WENT	WITH
HE	WENT	3:	WITH	ARMY	DOWN	HIS	6	JDT
6	HE	WITH	WENT	HIS	ARMY	JDT	3:	DOWN
3:	HIS	ARMY	DOWN	JDT	HE	6	WITH	WENT
WENT	DOWN	JDT	3:	WITH	6	HE	HIS	ARMY
ARMY	WITH	DOWN	HE	6	HIS	WENT	JDT	3:
HIS	3:	HE	JDT	DOWN	WENT	WITH	ARMY	6
JDT	6	WENT	ARMY	3:	WITH	DOWN	HE	HIS

21

GEBA	JDT	CAMP	SET	BETWEEN	3:10	HE	UP	HIS
SET	UP	HIS	CAMP	JDT	HE	GEBA	3:10	BETWEEN
3:10	HE	BETWEEN	UP	GEBA	HIS	SET	JDT	CAMP
BETWEEN	GEBA	SET	JDT	3:10	CAMP	UP	HIS	HE
UP	3:10	JDT	HIS	HE	SET	BETWEEN	CAMP	GEBA
HIS	CAMP	HE	GEBA	UP	BETWEEN	JDT	SET	3:10
HE	HIS	UP	3:10	SET	GEBA	CAMP	BETWEEN	JDT
CAMP	SET	GEBA	BETWEEN	HIS	JDT	3:10	HE	UP
JDT	BETWEEN	3:10	HE	CAMP	UP	HIS	GEBA	SET

22

OF	DREAD	4:2	WERE	JDT	EXTREME	THEY	HIM	IN
WERE	JDT	IN	THEY	OF	HIM	EXTREME	DREAD	4:2
EXTREME	THEY	HIM	IN	4:2	DREAD	WERE	JDT	OF
THEY	IN	JDT	DREAD	HIM	WERE	OF	4:2	EXTREME
DREAD	4:2	OF	EXTREME	IN	JDT	HIM	THEY	WERE
HIM	EXTREME	WERE	4:2	THEY	OF	DREAD	IN	JDT
IN	OF	EXTREME	HIM	DREAD	4:2	JDT	WERE	THEY
4:2	WERE	DREAD	JDT	EXTREME	THEY	IN	OF	HIM
JDT	HIM	THEY	OF	WERE	IN	4:2	EXTREME	DREAD

23

MEN	GOD	THE	CRIED	TO	OF	ISRAEL	JDT 4:9	ALL
ALL	TO	OF	MEN	ISRAEL	JDT 4:9	GOD	CRIED	THE
CRIED	JDT 4:9	ISRAEL	ALL	THE	GOD	MEN	TO	OF
ISRAEL	ALL	JDT 4:9	THE	CRIED	MEN	OF	GOD	TO
GOD	CRIED	TO	OF	JDT 4:9	ISRAEL	THE	ALL	MEN
THE	OF	MEN	GOD	ALL	TO	JDT 4:9	ISRAEL	CRIED
TO	ISRAEL	CRIED	JDT 4:9	OF	THE	ALL	MEN	GOD
OF	MEN	ALL	ISRAEL	GOD	CRIED	TO	THE	JDT 4:9
JDT 4:9	THE	GOD	TO	MEN	ALL	CRIED	OF	ISRAEL

24

AND	HEARD	REGARD	THEIR	JDT 4:13	THE	HAD	CRY	LORD
HAD	THE	JDT 4:13	CRY	AND	LORD	THEIR	HEARD	REGARD
CRY	THEIR	LORD	HAD	REGARD	HEARD	JDT 4:13	THE	AND
JDT 4:13	HAD	HEARD	AND	LORD	CRY	THE	REGARD	THEIR
LORD	REGARD	CRY	THE	THEIR	JDT 4:13	HEARD	AND	HAD
THEIR	AND	THE	REGARD	HEARD	HAD	LORD	JDT 4:13	CRY
REGARD	LORD	HAD	JDT 4:13	THE	AND	CRY	THEIR	HEARD
HEARD	JDT 4:13	AND	LORD	CRY	THEIR	REGARD	HAD	THE
THE	CRY	THEIR	HEARD	HAD	REGARD	AND	LORD	JDT 4:13

25

THEY	ALL	TO THE	WITH	CRIED	STRENGTH	JDT 4:15	LORD	THEIR
THEIR	WITH	LORD	JDT 4:15	THEY	TO THE	ALL	CRIED	STRENGTH
JDT 4:15	CRIED	STRENGTH	ALL	LORD	THEIR	WITH	TO THE	THEY
STRENGTH	TO THE	CRIED	LORD	THEIR	ALL	THEY	JDT. 4:15	WITH
ALL	LORD	JDT 4:15	THEY	STRENGTH	WITH	CRIED	THEIR	TO THE
WITH	THEIR	THEY	TO THE	JDT 4:15	CRIED	STRENGTH	ALL	LORD
CRIED	JDT 4:15	WITH	STRENGTH	TO THE	LORD	THEIR	THEY	ALL
LORD	THEY	ALL	THEIR	WITH	JDT 4:15	TO THE	STRENGTH	CRIED
TO THE	STRENGTH	THEIR	CRIED	ALL	THEY	LORD	WITH	JDT 4:15

26

SUMMONED	RULERS	GREAT	HE	THE	ANGER	JDT 5:2	ALL	IN
ALL	ANGER	THE	JDT 5:2	RULERS	IN	GREAT	SUMMONED	HE
IN	HE	JDT 5:2	SUMMONED	ALL	GREAT	ANGER	THE	RULERS
THE	GREAT	HE	ALL	ANGER	SUMMONED	IN	RULERS	JDT 5:2
ANGER	IN	RULERS	THE	JDT 5:2	HE	ALL	GREAT	SUMMONED
JDT 5:2	SUMMONED	ALL	GREAT	IN	RULERS	THE	HE	ANGER
HE	ALL	ANGER	IN	SUMMONED	THE	RULERS	JDT 5:2	GREAT
RULERS	THE	SUMMONED	ANGER	GREAT	JDT 5:2	HE	IN	ALL
GREAT	JDT 5:2	IN	RULERS	HE	ALL	SUMMONED	ANGER	THE

27

COME	5:4	OUT	HAVE	JDT	TO	REFUSED	THEY	WHY
TO	HAVE	REFUSED	WHY	OUT	THEY	JDT	COME	5:4
JDT	THEY	WHY	5:4	REFUSED	COME	OUT	HAVE	TO
WHY	OUT	COME	JDT	THEY	REFUSED	TO	5:4	HAVE
THEY	TO	5:4	OUT	HAVE	WHY	COME	JDT	REFUSED
HAVE	REFUSED	JDT	TO	COME	5:4	THEY	WHY	OUT
OUT	COME	TO	THEY	WHY	HAVE	5:4	REFUSED	JDT
5:4	WHY	THEY	REFUSED	TO	JDT	HAVE	OUT	COME
REFUSED	JDT	HAVE	COME	5:4	OUT	WHY	TO	THEY

28

GLOOMY	A:7	A	WAS	AND	ESTH	DAY	DARK	IT
DARK	IT	WAS	A:7	A	DAY	GLOOMY	AND	ESTH
ESTH	DAY	AND	GLOOMY	DARK	IT	WAS	A:7	A
AND	GLOOMY	ESTH	DARK	DAY	A:7	IT	A	WAS
A:7	DARK	DAY	A	IT	WAS	ESTH.	GLOOMY	AND
WAS	A	IT	AND	ESTH	GLOOMY	A:7	DAY	DARK
A	ESTH	A:7	IT	GLOOMY	AND	DARK	WAS	DAY
DAY	WAS	DARK	ESTH	A:7	A	AND	IT	GLOOMY
IT	AND	GLOOMY	DAY	WAS	DARK	A	ESTH	A:7

29

WHO	IS	RESIST	YOU	NO ONE	LORD	THERE	ESTH C:4	CAN
CAN	YOU	THERE	WHO	RESIST	ESTH C:4	IS	LORD	NO ONE
NO ONE	ESTH C:4	LORD	THERE	CAN	IS	WHO	YOU	RESIST
ESTH C:4	THERE	WHO	NO ONE	LORD	CAN	RESIST	IS	YOU
RESIST	NO ONE	IS	ESTH C:4	YOU	THERE	LORD	CAN	WHO
LORD	CAN	YOU	IS	WHO	RESIST	ESTH C:4	NO ONE	THERE
YOU	RESIST	ESTH C:4	CAN	IS	WHO	NO ONE	THERE	LORD
IS	WHO	NO ONE	LORD	THERE	YOU	CAN	RESIST	ESTH C:4
THERE	LORD	CAN	RESIST	ESTH C:4	NO ONE	YOU	WHO	IS

30

ESTH	B:9	INVOKE	SPEAK	TO	THE LORD	THE	AND	KING
SPEAK	THE LORD	KING	THE	AND	INVOKE	B:9	TO	ESTH
THE	TO	AND	B:9	KING	ESTH	SPEAK	INVOKE	THE LORD
INVOKE	KING	B:9	TO	ESTH	THE	AND	THE LORD	SPEAK
AND	ESTH	TO	THE LORD	SPEAK	KING	INVOKE	THE	B:9
THE LORD	SPEAK	THE	INVOKE	B:9	AND	ESTH	KING	TO
B:9	AND	SPEAK	KING	THE	TO	THE LORD	ESTH	INVOKE
KING	INVOKE	ESTH	AND	THE LORD	SPEAK	TO	B:9	THE
TO	THE	THE LORD	ESTH	INVOKE	B:9	KING	SPEAK	AND

31

STOOD	D:6	WITH	TO FACE	FACE	SHE	KING	ESTH	THE
FACE	ESTH	KING	THE	WITH	D:6	STOOD	SHE	TO FACE
TO FACE	SHE	THE	ESTH	KING	STOOD	FACE	D:6	WITH
KING	WITH	ESTH	FACE	SHE	TO FACE	THE	STOOD	D:6
SHE	THE	STOOD	WITH	D:6	KING	ESTH	TO FACE	FACE
D:6	FACE	TO FACE	STOOD	ESTH	THE	SHE	WITH	KING
ESTH	KING	D:6	SHE	THE	WITH	TO FACE	FACE	STOOD
THE	STOOD	SHE	D:6	TO FACE	FACE	WITH	KING	ESTH
WITH	TO FACE	FACE	KING	STOOD	ESTH	D:6	THE	SHE

32

THE KING	IS	RIVER	THE	ESTH	WHOM	F:3	MARRIED	ESTHER
THE	WHOM	MARRIED	ESTHER	F:3	RIVER	ESTH	IS	THE KING
ESTH	ESTHER	F:3	IS	MARRIED	THE KING	RIVER	THE	WHOM
F:3	MARRIED	IS	THE KING	WHOM	ESTHER	THE	RIVER	ESTH
ESTHER	RIVER	THE KING	ESTH	IS	THE	WHOM	F:3	MARRIED
WHOM	ESTH	THE	MARRIED	RIVER	F:3	ESTHER	THE KING	IS
IS	THE KING	ESTHER	F:3	THE	ESTH	MARRIED	WHOM	RIVER
RIVER	THE	ESTH	WHOM	THE KING	MARRIED	IS	ESTHER	F:3
MARRIED	F:3	WHOM	RIVER	ESTHER	IS	THE KING	ESTH	THE

33

ABRAHAM	1 MACC	FOUND	WAS	2:52	FAITHFUL	TRIAL	IN	NOT
WAS	TRIAL	IN	NOT	ABRAHAM	1 MACC	FOUND	2:52	FAITHFUL
FAITHFUL	2:52	NOT	IN	FOUND	TRIAL	ABRAHAM	WAS	1 MACC
2:52	ABRAHAM	1 MACC	TRIAL	FAITHFUL	IN	NOT	FOUND	WAS
TRIAL	NOT	WAS	2:52	1 MACC	FOUND	FAITHFUL	ABRAHAM	IN
FOUND	IN	FAITHFUL	ABRAHAM	NOT	WAS	2:52	1 MACC	TRIAL
1 MACC	FAITHFUL	2:52	FOUND	IN	NOT	WAS	TRIAL	ABRAHAM
IN	FOUND	TRIAL	FAITHFUL	WAS	ABRAHAM	1 MACC	NOT	2:52
NOT	WAS	ABRAHAM	1 MACC	TRIAL	2:52	IN	FAITHFUL	FOUND

34

MAN	WORDS	A	DO NOT	OF	THE	1 MACC 2:62	SINFUL	FEAR
SINFUL	OF	DO NOT	FEAR	A	1 MACC 2:62	THE	WORDS	MAN
1 MACC 2:62	FEAR	THE	SINFUL	MAN	WORDS	OF	A	DO NOT
FEAR	MAN	OF	WORDS	THE	DO NOT	A	1 MACC 2:62	SINFUL
DO NOT	SINFUL	WORDS	A	1 MACC 2:62	MAN	FEAR	OF	THE
A	THE	1 MACC 2:62	OF	SINFUL	FEAR	MAN	DO NOT	WORDS
THE	A	SINFUL	MAN	WORDS	OF	DO NOT	FEAR	1 MACC 2:62
WORDS	1 MACC 2:62	FEAR	THE	DO NOT	A	SINFUL	MAN	OF
OF	DO NOT	MAN	1 MACC 2:62	FEAR	SINFUL	WORDS	THE	A

35

THE	IN	3:1	HOLY	PEACE	PERFECT	2 MACC	CITY	LIVED
LIVED	PEACE	PERFECT	THE	2 MACC	CITY	HOLY	IN	3:1
HOLY	2 MACC	CITY	LIVED	3:1	IN	THE	PEACE	PERFECT
3:1	CITY	THE	PEACE	LIVED	2 MACC	PERFECT	HOLY	IN
2 MACC	HOLY	IN	3:1	PERFECT	THE	PEACE	LIVED	CITY
PEACE	PERFECT	LIVED	CITY	IN	HOLY	3:1	THE	2 MACC
IN	3:1	PEACE	2 MACC	HOLY	LIVED	CITY	PERFECT	THE
CITY	LIVED	HOLY	PERFECT	THE	3:1	IN	2 MACC	PEACE
PERFECT	THE	2 MACC	IN	CITY	PEACE	LIVED	3:1	HOLY

36

SPIRIT	FILLS	LORD	1:7	WORLD	THE	FOR THE	OF THE	WIS
WORLD	1:7	FOR THE	LORD	WIS	OF THE	SPIRIT	THE	FILLS
THE	OF THE	WIS	SPIRIT	FILLS	FOR THE	WORLD	LORD	1:7
LORD	FOR THE	THE	WORLD	SPIRIT	FILLS	WIS	1:7	OF THE
1:7	SPIRIT	OF THE	FOR THE	THE	WIS	FILLS	WORLD	LORD
WIS	WORLD	FILLS	OF THE	LORD	1:7	THE	FOR THE	SPIRIT
FILLS	WIS	1:7	THE	OF THE	WORLD	LORD	SPIRIT	FOR THE
OF THE	THE	SPIRIT	FILLS	FOR THE	LORD	1:7	WIS	WORLD
FOR THE	LORD	WORLD	WIS	1:7	SPIRIT	OF THE	FILLS	THE

37

WHO	EARTH	JUDGE	1:1	JUSTICE	WIS	THE	YOU	LOVE
YOU	THE	1:1	JUDGE	LOVE	EARTH	WIS	JUSTICE	WHO
LOVE	JUSTICE	WIS	WHO	THE	YOU	JUDGE	1:1	EARTH
1:1	LOVE	WHO	JUSTICE	JUDGE	THE	EARTH	WIS	YOU
WIS	JUDGE	THE	YOU	EARTH	LOVE	1:1	WHO	JUSTICE
JUSTICE	YOU	EARTH	WIS	WHO	1:1	LOVE	JUDGE	THE
THE	WHO	YOU	LOVE	1:1	JUDGE	JUSTICE	EARTH	WIS
JUDGE	WIS	LOVE	EARTH	YOU	JUSTICE	WHO	THE	1:1
EARTH	1:1	JUSTICE	THE	WIS	WHO	YOU	LOVE	JUDGE

38

WISDOM	ENTERS	PLOTS	NOT	EVIL	WIS 1:4	INTO	A SOUL	THAT
NOT	A SOUL	THAT	PLOTS	ENTERS	INTO	WISDOM	WIS 1:4	EVIL
WIS 1:4	INTO	EVIL	A SOUL	WISDOM	THAT	NOT	ENTERS	PLOTS
EVIL	WISDOM	NOT	ENTERS	WIS 1:4	PLOTS	A SOUL	THAT	INTO
A SOUL	WIS 1:4	ENTERS	THAT	INTO	NOT	EVIL	PLOTS	WISDOM
THAT	PLOTS	INTO	WISDOM	A SOUL	EVIL	ENTERS	NOT	WIS 1:4
INTO	THAT	A SOUL	WIS 1:4	NOT	WISDOM	PLOTS	EVIL	ENTERS
PLOTS	NOT	WISDOM	EVIL	THAT	ENTERS	WIS 1:4	INTO	A SOUL
ENTERS	EVIL	WIS 1:4	INTO	PLOTS	A SOUL	THAT	WISDOM	NOT

39

OUR	LIFETIME	SHADOW	PASSING	A	IS THE	WIS 2:5	OF	FOR
PASSING	WIS 2:5	IS THE	LIFETIME	FOR	OF	OUR	SHADOW	A
FOR	A	OF	WIS 2:5	SHADOW	OUR	PASSING	IS THE	LIFETIME
OF	SHADOW	LIFETIME	OUR	PASSING	A	IS THE	FOR	WIS 2:5
IS THE	OUR	A	SHADOW	WIS 2:5	FOR	OF	LIFETIME	PASSING
WIS 2:5	FOR	PASSING	OF	IS THE	LIFETIME	SHADOW	A	OUR
LIFETIME	IS THE	OUR	FOR	OF	PASSING	A	WIS 2:5	SHADOW
SHADOW	OF	FOR	A	OUR	WIS 2:5	LIFETIME	PASSING	IS THE
A	PASSING	WIS 2:5	IS THE	LIFETIME	SHADOW	FOR	OUR	OF

40

MOUTH	THE	LYING	SOUL	1:11	WIS	AND	SLAYS	A
AND	WIS	SOUL	A	SLAYS	MOUTH	THE	1:11	LYING
1:11	SLAYS	A	LYING	THE	AND	SOUL	WIS	MOUTH
SOUL	LYING	SLAYS	THE	WIS	1:11	MOUTH	A	AND
A	MOUTH	AND	SLAYS	LYING	SOUL	WIS	THE	1:11
WIS	1:11	THE	AND	MOUTH	A	SLAYS	LYING	SOUL
SLAYS	SOUL	1:11	WIS	AND	LYING	A	MOUTH	THE
THE	A	MOUTH	1:11	SOUL	SLAYS	LYING	AND	WIS
LYING	AND	WIS	MOUTH	A	THE	1:11	SOUL	SLAYS

41

WITH	SAINTS	WIS	5:5	THE	LOT	IS	HOW	HIS
THE	LOT	5:5	IS	HOW	HIS	WIS	WITH	SAINTS
IS	HIS	HOW	SAINTS	WIS	WITH	LOT	THE	5:5
5:5	WIS	LOT	THE	WITH	IS	SAINTS	HIS	HOW
SAINTS	HOW	IS	HIS	LOT	5:5	WITH	WIS	THE
HIS	THE	WITH	WIS	SAINTS	HOW	5:5	IS	LOT
WIS	IS	SAINTS	HOW	5:5	THE	HIS	LOT	WITH
LOT	5:5	THE	WITH	HIS	WIS	HOW	SAINTS	IS
HOW	WITH	HIS	LOT	IS	SAINTS	THE	5:5	WIS

42

NOT	WIS 5:6	DID	RISE	AND	SUN	FOR	THE	US
AND	US	FOR	THE	NOT	WIS 5:6	RISE	DID	SUN
SUN	RISE	THE	US	DID	FOR	AND	NOT	WIS 5:6
WIS 5:6	AND	US	FOR	THE	NOT	SUN	RISE	DID
THE	NOT	RISE	DID	SUN	US	WIS 5:6	FOR	AND
DID	FOR	SUN	AND	WIS 5:6	RISE	THE	US	NOT
FOR	SUN	WIS 5:6	NOT	US	THE	DID	AND	RISE
RISE	DID	NOT	SUN	FOR	AND	US	WIS 5:6	THE
US	THE	AND	WIS 5:6	RISE	DID	NOT	SUN	FOR

43

YOU	AND	NOT	MAY	WIS 6:9	SIN	THAT	WISDOM	LEARN
WIS 6:9	THAT	LEARN	WISDOM	NOT	YOU	AND	SIN	MAY
MAY	SIN	WISDOM	LEARN	AND	THAT	YOU	NOT	WIS 6:9
LEARN	NOT	AND	YOU	MAY	WISDOM	SIN	WIS 6:9	THAT
THAT	WIS 6:9	SIN	NOT	LEARN	AND	WISDOM	MAY	YOU
WISDOM	MAY	YOU	SIN	THAT	WIS 6:9	LEARN	AND	NOT
NOT	WISDOM	MAY	THAT	SIN	LEARN	WIS 6:9	YOU	AND
SIN	LEARN	WIS 6:9	AND	YOU	NOT	MAY	THAT	WISDOM
AND	YOU	THAT	WIS 6:9	WISDOM	MAY	NOT	LEARN	SIN

44

AFTER	YOUTH	AND	I LOVED	FROM	HER	SOUGHT	MY	WIS 8:2
I LOVED	FROM	SOUGHT	YOUTH	WIS 8:2	MY	HER	AND	AFTER
WIS 8:2	MY	HER	AND	SOUGHT	AFTER	YOUTH	I LOVED	FROM
HER	WIS 8:2	FROM	AFTER	YOUTH	AND	MY	SOUGHT	I LOVED
SOUGHT	AND	I LOVED	MY	HER	WIS 8:2	AFTER	FROM	YOUTH
YOUTH	AFTER	MY	FROM	I LOVED	SOUGHT	WIS 8:2	HER	AND
AND	HER	YOUTH	SOUGHT	AFTER	FROM	I LOVED	WIS 8:2	MY
FROM	I LOVED	WIS 8:2	HER	MY	YOUTH	AND	AFTER	SOUGHT
MY	SOUGHT	AFTER	WIS 8:2	AND	I LOVED	FROM	YOUTH	HER

45

7:	IS	GOD	28	LOVES	NOUGHT	THERE	FOR	WIS
THERE	28	FOR	WIS	IS	GOD	LOVES	NOUGHT	7:
WIS	LOVES	NOUGHT	7:	FOR	THERE	28	GOD	IS
FOR	GOD	LOVES	IS	28	7:	NOUGHT	WIS	THERE
28	WIS	THERE	NOUGHT	GOD	LOVES	7:	IS	FOR
NOUGHT	7:	IS	FOR	THERE	WIS	GOD	28	LOVES
LOVES	FOR	WIS	GOD	7:	28	IS	THERE	NOUGHT
IS	THERE	28	LOVES	NOUGHT	FOR	WIS	7:	GOD
GOD	NOUGHT	7:	THERE	WIS	IS	FOR	LOVES	28

46

THAN	WIS	FAIRER	7:29	FOR	IS	THE	SHE	SUN
THE	7:29	SUN	SHE	WIS	THAN	FOR	FAIRER	IS
SHE	IS	FOR	SUN	THE	FAIRER	THAN	WIS	7:29
7:29	SHE	THAN	FAIRER	SUN	THE	IS	FOR	WIS
WIS	FAIRER	THE	FOR	IS	SHE	SUN	7:29	THAN
FOR	SUN	IS	THAN	7:29	WIS	FAIRER	THE	SHE
FAIRER	THE	WIS	IS	THAN	7:29	SHE	SUN	FOR
SUN	THAN	SHE	WIS	FAIRER	FOR	7:29	IS	THE
IS	FOR	7:29	THE	SHE	SUN	WIS	THAN	FAIRER

47

OUR	DID	PRIDE	WIS	WHAT	8	US	AVAIL	5:
US	WIS	8	5:	PRIDE	AVAIL	WHAT	DID	OUR
AVAIL	5:	WHAT	OUR	DID	US	8	WIS	PRIDE
DID	8	AVAIL	PRIDE	US	WHAT	5:	OUR	WIS
WIS	WHAT	OUR	8	AVAIL	5:	DID	PRIDE	US
5:	PRIDE	US	DID	WIS	OUR	AVAIL	8	WHAT
8	US	WIS	AVAIL	5:	PRIDE	OUR	WHAT	DID
WHAT	OUR	DID	US	8	WIS	PRIDE	5:	AVAIL
PRIDE	AVAIL	5:	WHAT	OUR	DID	WIS	US	8

48

FAVORED	WIS	NOW	CHILD	WAS	A	I	WELL	8:19
CHILD	WELL	WAS	I	8:19	NOW	WIS	FAVORED	A
A	8:19	I	FAVORED	WIS	WELL	CHILD	WAS	NOW
WIS	I	A	WAS	NOW	FAVORED	8:19	CHILD	WELL
8:19	NOW	CHILD	A	WELL	I	WAS	WIS	FAVORED
WELL	WAS	FAVORED	WIS	CHILD	8:19	A	NOW	I
NOW	CHILD	8:19	WELL	I	WIS	FAVORED	A	WAS
I	FAVORED	WIS	NOW	A	WAS	WELL	8:19	CHILD
WAS	A	WELL	8:19	FAVORED	CHILD	NOW	I	WIS

49

THE	THRONE	YOUR	WISDOM	AT	ATTENDANT	ME	WIS 9:4	GIVE
WIS 9:4	WISDOM	ATTENDANT	THRONE	GIVE	ME	AT	YOUR	THE
AT	ME	GIVE	WIS 9:4	YOUR	THE	WISDOM	ATTENDANT	THRONE
YOUR	ATTENDANT	WIS 9:4	THE	WISDOM	THRONE	GIVE	ME	AT
WISDOM	THE	ME	AT	ATTENDANT	GIVE	YOUR	THRONE	WIS 9:4
THRONE	GIVE	AT	YOUR	ME	WIS 9:4	THE	WISDOM	ATTENDANT
ME	WIS 9:4	THE	GIVE	THRONE	WISDOM	ATTENDANT	AT	YOUR
GIVE	YOUR	WISDOM	ATTENDANT	WIS 9:4	AT	THRONE	THE	ME
ATTENDANT	AT	THRONE	ME	THE	YOUR	WIS 9:4	GIVE	WISDOM

50

IN	KEEL	WAVES	THE	ITS	WIS 5:10	PATH	NO	OF
THE	PATH	NO	WAVES	OF	KEEL	IN	ITS	WIS 5:10
ITS	OF	WIS 5:10	NO	IN	PATH	THE	WAVES	KEEL
PATH	WAVES	OF	KEEL	NO	THE	WIS 5:10	IN	ITS
NO	WIS 5:10	ITS	IN	PATH	OF	WAVES	KEEL	THE
KEEL	THE	IN	ITS	WIS 5:10	WAVES	NO	OF	PATH
WAVES	ITS	KEEL	WIS 5:10	THE	IN	OF	PATH	NO
WIS 5:10	IN	PATH	OF	KEEL	NO	ITS	THE	WAVES
OF	NO	THE	PATH	WAVES	ITS	KEEL	WIS 5:10	IN

51

WHO	HE	WATCHES	DAWN	FOR	6:14	HER	WIS	AT
HER	6:14	AT	WATCHES	WIS	WHO	DAWN	FOR	HE
FOR	WIS	DAWN	HER	AT	HE	6:14	WATCHES	WHO
6:14	FOR	WIS	AT	WHO	WATCHES	HE	HER	DAWN
DAWN	AT	WHO	HE	HER	FOR	WATCHES	6:14	WIS
WATCHES	HER	HE	6:14	DAWN	WIS	WHO	AT	FOR
AT	WATCHES	HER	FOR	HE	DAWN	WIS	WHO	6:14
WIS	DAWN	6:14	WHO	WATCHES	AT	FOR	HE	HER
HE	WHO	FOR	WIS	6:14	HER	AT	DAWN	WATCHES

52

KNOWS	SHE	ALL	WIS	THINGS	FOR	UNDER-STANDS	AND	9:11
AND	THINGS	9:11	UNDER-STANDS	ALL	KNOWS	SHE	FOR	WIS
FOR	WIS	UNDER-STANDS	AND	SHE	9:11	KNOWS	ALL	THINGS
UNDER-STANDS	AND	WIS	THINGS	KNOWS	ALL	9:11	SHE	FOR
THINGS	ALL	FOR	SHE	9:11	WIS	AND	KNOWS	UNDER-STANDS
SHE	9:11	KNOWS	FOR	UNDER-STANDS	AND	WIS	THINGS	ALL
WIS	UNDER-STANDS	AND	ALL	FOR	SHE	THINGS	9:11	KNOWS
9:11	FOR	SHE	KNOWS	WIS	THINGS	ALL	UNDER-STANDS	AND
ALL	KNOWS	THINGS	9:11	AND	UNDER-STANDS	FOR	WIS	SHE

53

MAN	WIS	NOT	THE	DID	SHE	10:13	JUST	ABANDON
ABANDON	SHE	DID	10:13	JUST	WIS	NOT	MAN	THE
THE	10:13	JUST	NOT	MAN	ABANDON	SHE	DID	WIS
10:13	ABANDON	MAN	DID	WIS	NOT	JUST	THE	SHE
WIS	JUST	SHE	MAN	10:13	THE	ABANDON	NOT	DID
DID	NOT	THE	ABANDON	SHE	JUST	WIS	10:13	MAN
JUST	THE	ABANDON	SHE	NOT	MAN	DID	WIS	10:13
NOT	MAN	10:13	WIS	ABANDON	DID	THE	SHE	JUST
SHE	DID	WIS	JUST	THE	10:13	MAN	ABANDON	NOT

54

WIS 10:8	OF	MEMORIAL	LEFT	THEIR	MANKIND	FOLLY	A	THEY
FOLLY	LEFT	THEY	WIS 10:8	MEMORIAL	A	THEIR	MANKIND	OF
A	THEIR	MANKIND	FOLLY	OF	THEY	LEFT	WIS 10:8	MEMORIAL
MANKIND	WIS 10:8	THEIR	MEMORIAL	LEFT	FOLLY	OF	THEY	A
THEY	FOLLY	OF	A	WIS 10:8	THEIR	MANKIND	MEMORIAL	LEFT
LEFT	MEMORIAL	A	MANKIND	THEY	OF	WIS 10:8	THEIR	FOLLY
MEMORIAL	A	LEFT	THEIR	FOLLY	WIS 10:8	THEY	OF	MANKIND
OF	MANKIND	WIS 10:8	THEY	A	LEFT	MEMORIAL	FOLLY	THEIR
THEIR	THEY	FOLLY	OF	MANKIND	MEMORIAL	A	LEFT	WIS 10:8

55

WICKED	THEIR	FOR	RETURN	THOUGHTS	WIS 11:15	IN	SENSELESS	AND
WIS 11:15	IN	RETURN	AND	THEIR	SENSELESS	WICKED	THOUGHTS	FOR
SENSELESS	AND	THOUGHTS	WICKED	FOR	IN	WIS 11:15	THEIR	RETURN
AND	WICKED	WIS 11:15	THOUGHTS	IN	THEIR	RETURN	FOR	SENSELESS
FOR	THOUGHTS	SENSELESS	WIS 11:15	AND	RETURN	THEIR	IN	WICKED
IN	RETURN	THEIR	SENSELESS	WICKED	FOR	AND	WIS 11:15	THOUGHTS
THOUGHTS	FOR	IN	THEIR	RETURN	WICKED	SENSELESS	AND	WIS 11:15
THEIR	SENSELESS	WICKED	FOR	WIS 11:15	AND	THOUGHTS	RETURN	IN
RETURN	WIS 11:15	AND	IN	SENSELESS	THOUGHTS	FOR	WICKED	THEIR

56

THE	THAT	YOU WILL	PRODUCTS	NOT IDLE	BE	WISDOM	WIS 14:5	OF YOUR
WIS 14:5	OF YOUR	PRODUCTS	YOU WILL	WISDOM	THAT	NOT IDLE	THE	BE
NOT IDLE	BE	WISDOM	OF YOUR	WIS 14:5	THE	THAT	PRODUCTS	YOU WILL
YOU WILL	WIS 14:5	THE	BE	OF YOUR	NOT IDLE	PRODUCTS	THAT	WISDOM
THAT	NOT IDLE	BE	THE	PRODUCTS	WISDOM	YOU WILL	OF YOUR	WIS 14:5
WISDOM	PRODUCTS	OF YOUR	THAT	YOU WILL	WIS 14:5	THE	BE	NOT IDLE
OF YOUR	THE	THAT	WISDOM	BE	YOU WILL	WIS 14:5	NOT IDLE	PRODUCTS
BE	YOU WILL	NOT IDLE	WIS 14:5	THE	PRODUCTS	OF YOUR	WISDOM	THAT
PRODUCTS	WISDOM	WIS 14:5	NOT IDLE	THAT	OF YOUR	BE	YOU WILL	THE

57

FOR	ALWAYS	WITH	GREAT	11:21	YOU	STRENGTH	ABIDES	WIS
YOU	STRENGTH	ABIDES	WITH	WIS	ALWAYS	11:21	FOR	GREAT
GREAT	11:21	WIS	FOR	STRENGTH	ABIDES	WITH	ALWAYS	YOU
STRENGTH	ABIDES	GREAT	11:21	YOU	WITH	ALWAYS	WIS	FOR
WITH	WIS	YOU	STRENGTH	ALWAYS	FOR	GREAT	11:21	ABIDES
ALWAYS	FOR	11:21	WIS	ABIDES	GREAT	YOU	WITH	STRENGTH
11:21	WITH	STRENGTH	YOU	FOR	WIS	ABIDES	GREAT	ALWAYS
ABIDES	GREAT	FOR	ALWAYS	WITH	STRENGTH	WIS	YOU	11:21
WIS	YOU	ALWAYS	ABIDES	GREAT	11:21	FOR	STRENGTH	WITH

58

HOW	POWERFUL	IS HE	MADE	WIS 13:4	WHO	THEM	MORE	MUCH
MADE	THEM	MUCH	MORE	POWERFUL	HOW	WHO	IS HE	WIS 13:4
WIS 13:4	WHO	MORE	IS HE	MUCH	THEM	MADE	POWERFUL	HOW
POWRFUL	HOW	THEM	WHO	MADE	MUCH	IS HE	WIS 13:4	MORE
MUCH	WIS 13:4	WHO	POWERFUL	MORE	IS HE	HOW	THEM	MADE
IS HE	MORE	MADE	HOW	THEM	WIS 13:4	POWERFUL	MUCH	WHO
THEM	MUCH	HOW	WIS 13:4	WHO	POWERFUL	MORE	MADE	IS HE
WHO	MADE	POWERFUL	MUCH	IS HE	MORE	WIS. 13:4	HOW	THEM
MORE	IS HE	WIS 13:4	THEM	HOW	MADE	MUCH	WHO	POWERFUL

59

MEN	WERE	EVEN	AS	THESE	THEY	BUT	12:8	WIS
BUT	AS	12:8	WIS	WERE	EVEN	THESE	THEY	MEN
THEY	THESE	WIS	12:8	BUT	MEN	WERE	EVEN	AS
WERE	BUT	THEY	MEN	AS	12:8	EVEN	WIS	THESE
THESE	WIS	MEN	EVEN	THEY	WERE	12:8	AS	BUT
EVEN	12:8	AS	THESE	WIS	BUT	MEN	WERE	THEY
WIS	MEN	WERE	THEY	12:8	THESE	AS	BUT	EVEN
12:8	THEY	THESE	BUT	EVEN	AS	WIS	MEN	WERE
AS	EVEN	BUT	WERE	MEN	WIS	THEY	THESE	12:8

60

WIS 15:1	YOU	GOD	TRUE	ARE	OUR	BUT	AND	GOOD
GOOD	ARE	OUR	BUT	GOD	AND	TRUE	WIS 15:1	YOU
TRUE	BUT	AND	GOOD	WIS 15:1	YOU	OUR	ARE	GOD
AND	GOOD	YOU	WIS 15:1	OUR	ARE	GOD	BUT	TRUE
OUR	WIS 15:1	BUT	GOD	TRUE	GOOD	ARE	YOU	AND
GOD	TRUE	ARE	YOU	AND	BUT	GOOD	OUR	WIS 15:1
YOU	GOD	TRUE	OUR	BUT	WIS 15:1	AND	GOOD	ARE
BUT	AND	WIS 15:1	ARE	GOOD	GOD	YOU	TRUE	OUR
ARE	OUR	GOOD	AND	YOU	TRUE	WIS 15:1	GOD	BUT

61

14:13	IN	THE	BEGINNING	THEY	WERE	NOT	WIS	FOR
WIS	BEGINNING	NOT	FOR	IN	THE	THEY	WERE	14:13
FOR	THEY	WERE	WIS	NOT	14:13	IN	THE	BEGINNING
WERE	THE	BEGINNING	IN	14:13	NOT	FOR	THEY	WIS
IN	FOR	WIS	THEY	WERE	BEGINNING	14:13	NOT	THE
NOT	14:13	THEY	THE	WIS	FOR	WERE	BEGINNING	IN
THE	NOT	IN	14:13	BEGINNING	THEY	WIS	FOR	WERE
THEY	WIS	FOR	WERE	THE	IN	BEGINNING	14:13	NOT
BEGINNING	WERE	14:13	NOT	FOR	WIS	THE	IN	THEY

62

16:	ESCAPE	HAND	15	CAN	BUT	YOUR	WIS	NONE
15	NONE	CAN	YOUR	WIS	ESCAPE	16:	HAND	BUT
BUT	YOUR	WIS	NONE	16:	HAND	ESCAPE	15	CAN
WIS	16:	NONE	CAN	ESCAPE	YOUR	15	BUT	HAND
HAND	15	YOUR	WIS	BUT	16:	CAN	NONE	ESCAPE
ESCAPE	CAN	BUT	HAND	NONE	15	WIS	16:	YOUR
CAN	HAND	15	BUT	YOUR	WIS	NONE	ESCAPE	16:
YOUR	BUT	ESCAPE	16:	15	NONE	HAND	CAN	WIS
NONE	WIS	16:	ESCAPE	HAND	CAN	BUT	YOUR	15

63

BUT	LIGHT	HAD	VERY	GREAT	HOLY	WIS 18:1	ONES	YOUR
GREAT	ONES	VERY	HAD	WIS 18:1	YOUR	LIGHT	BUT	HOLY
WIS 18:1	HOLY	YOUR	ONES	BUT	LIGHT	GREAT	HAD	VERY
HOLY	VERY	GREAT	LIGHT	ONES	HAD	BUT	YOUR	WIS 18:1
YOUR	BUT	WIS 18:1	HOLY	VERY	GREAT	ONES	LIGHT	HAD
ONES	HAD	LIGHT	WIS 18:1	YOUR	BUT	VERY	HOLY	GREAT
LIGHT	GREAT	ONES	YOUR	HOLY	WIS 18:1	HAD	VERY	BUT
HAD	WIS 18:1	HOLY	BUT	LIGHT	VERY	YOUR	GREAT	ONES
VERY	YOUR	BUT	GREAT	HAD	ONES	HOLY	WIS 18:1	LIGHT

64

THEY	KNEW	WERE	YET	BEFORE-HAND	FOR HE	WIS 19:1	TO DO	WHAT
WIS 19:1	YET	FOR HE	TO DO	WHAT	WERE	KNEW	THEY	BEFORE-HAND
BEFORE-HAND	WHAT	TO DO	THEY	WIS 19:1	KNEW	YET	WERE	FOR HE
WERE	FOR HE	THEY	KNEW	TO DO	WIS 19:1	WHAT	BEFORE-HAND	YET
WHAT	TO DO	WIS 19:1	WERE	YET	BEFORE-HAND	THEY	FOR HE	KNEW
KNEW	BEFORE-HAND	YET	FOR HE	THEY	WHAT	TO DO	WIS 19:1	WERE
FOR HE	WIS 19:1	WHAT	BEFORE-HAND	KNEW	THEY	WERE	YET	TO DO
TO DO	WERE	KNEW	WIS 19:1	FOR HE	YET	BEFORE-HAND	WHAT	THEY
YET	THEY	BEFORE-HAND	WHAT	WERE	TO DO	FOR HE	KNEW	WIS 19:1

65

SIR 28:26	CARE	NOT	TO	SLIP	BY	YOUR	TONGUE	TAKE
TONGUE	TO	YOUR	TAKE	CARE	NOT	SLIP	BY	SIR 28:26
TAKE	SLIP	BY	TONGUE	YOUR	SIR 28:26	CARE	NOT	TO
BY	NOT	TO	CARE	SIR 28:26	YOUR	TAKE	SLIP	TONGUE
CARE	TAKE	TONGUE	SLIP	BY	TO	SIR 28:26	YOUR	NOT
YOUR	SIR 28:26	SLIP	NOT	TONGUE	TAKE	BY	TO	CARE
NOT	YOUR	CARE	SIR 28:26	TO	SLIP	TONGUE	TAKE	BY
SLIP	TONGUE	TAKE	BY	NOT	CARE	TO	SIR 28:26	YOUR
TO	BY	SIR 28:26	YOUR	TAKE	TONGUE	NOT	CARE	SLIP

66

ALL	LORD	WISDOM	SIR	1	FROM	COMES	THE	1:
SIR	THE	1:	WISDOM	LORD	COMES	1	ALL	FROM
COMES	FROM	1	ALL	THE	1:	SIR	LORD	WISDOM
LORD	COMES	ALL	1:	WISDOM	THE	FROM	1	SIR
THE	WISDOM	SIR	COMES	FROM	1	ALL	1:	LORD
1	1:	FROM	LORD	ALL	SIR	WISDOM	COMES	THE
1:	SIR	LORD	1	COMES	WISDOM	THE	FROM	ALL
WISDOM	1	THE	FROM	1:	ALL	LORD	SIR	COMES
FROM	ALL	COMES	THE	SIR	LORD	1:	WISDOM	1

67

SERVE	MY SON	TO	YOU	COME	LORD	WHEN	THE	SIR 2:1
LORD	THE	WHEN	SERVE	SIR 2:1	MY SON	TO	YOU	COME
YOU	COME	SIR 2:1	THE	TO	WHEN	MY SON	SERVE	LORD
TO	SIR 2:1	LORD	WHEN	YOU	COME	SERVE	MY SON	THE
MY SON	SERVE	THE	TO	LORD	SIR 2:1	YOU	COME	WHEN
WHEN	YOU	COME	MY SON	THE	SERVE	LORD	SIR 2:1	TO
THE	TO	MY SON	COME	WHEN	YOU	SIR 2:1	LORD	SERVE
COME	LORD	SERVE	SIR 2:1	MY SON	TO	THE	WHEN	YOU
SIR 2:1	WHEN	YOU	LORD	SERVE	THE	COME	TO	MY SON

68

A	YOUR	AVERT	FROM	COMELY	9:8	EYES	SIR	WOMAN
9:8	WOMAN	EYES	YOUR	SIR	A	COMELY	AVERT	FROM
FROM	COMELY	SIR	AVERT	WOMAN	EYES	A	9:8	YOUR
COMELY	FROM	WOMAN	SIR	A	YOUR	AVERT	EYES	9:8
EYES	A	YOUR	WOMAN	9:8	AVERT	FROM	COMELY	SIR
AVERT	SIR	9:8	EYES	FROM	COMELY	WOMAN	YOUR	A
WOMAN	AVERT	FROM	9:8	EYES	SIR	YOUR	A	COMELY
YOUR	9:8	A	COMELY	AVERT	FROM	SIR	WOMAN	EYES
SIR	EYES	COMELY	A	YOUR	WOMAN	9:8	FROM	AVERT

69

FOR	SIR	PRIDE	OF	THE	10:13	IS	RESERVOIR	SIN
SIN	IS	THE	RESERVOIR	FOR	SIR	PRIDE	10:13	OF
OF	10:13	RESERVOIR	IS	PRIDE	SIN	FOR	THE	SIR
IS	FOR	10:13	SIR	SIN	PRIDE	RESERVOIR	OF	THE
THE	OF	SIR	FOR	IS	RESERVOIR	SIN	PRIDE	10:13
RESERVOIR	PRIDE	SIN	THE	10:13	OF	SIR	IS	FOR
SIR	THE	OF	SIN	RESERVOIR	IS	10:13	FOR	PRIDE
10:13	SIN	IS	PRIDE	OF	FOR	THE	SIR	RESERVOIR
PRIDE	RESERVOIR	FOR	10:13	SIR	THE	OF	SIN	IS

70

HIS	WHO	FEARS	HONORS	THE	HE	SIR 3:7	FATHER	LORD
HONORS	LORD	THE	FEARS	FATHER	SIR 3:7	HIS	HE	WHO
FATHER	SIR 3:7	HE	LORD	HIS	WHO	FEARS	HONORS	THE
WHO	HONORS	SIR 3:7	HE	LORD	THE	FATHER	FEARS	HIS
FEARS	HIS	LORD	SIR 3:7	HONORS	FATHER	WHO	THE	HE
THE	HE	FATHER	WHO	FEARS	HIS	HONORS	LORD	SIR 3:7
LORD	FATHER	WHO	THE	SIR 3:7	FEARS	HE	HIS	HONORS
SIR 3:7	THE	HIS	FATHER	HE	HONORS	LORD	WHO	FEARS
HE	FEARS	HONORS	HIS	WHO	LORD	THE	SIR 3:7	FATHER

71

SIR	A	NOT	7:8	DO	REPEAT	PLOT	SIN	TO
DO	PLOT	TO	SIR	NOT	SIN	7:8	A	REPEAT
REPEAT	7:8	SIN	TO	PLOT	A	DO	NOT	SIR
A	REPEAT	7:8	NOT	SIN	PLOT	TO	SIR	DO
TO	NOT	PLOT	A	SIR	DO	REPEAT	7:8	SIN
SIN	SIR	DO	REPEAT	7:8	TO	A	PLOT	NOT
PLOT	SIN	A	DO	TO	SIR	NOT	REPEAT	7:8
NOT	DO	REPEAT	SIN	A	7:8	SIR	TO	PLOT
7:8	TO	SIR	PLOT	REPEAT	NOT	SIN	DO	A

72

IF YOU	CAN	WISH	SON	TAUGHT	MY	YOU	SIR 6:32	BE
TAUGHT	SIR 6:32	SON	YOU	CAN	BE	MY	WISH	IF YOU
MY	BE	YOU	IF YOU	SIR 6:32	WISH	CAN	SON	TAUGHT
YOU	TAUGHT	MY	BE	SON	IF YOU	WISH	CAN	SIR 6:32
WISH	IF YOU	CAN	SIR 6:32	MY	TAUGHT	BE	YOU	SON
BE	SON	SIR 6:32	CAN	WISH	YOU	IF YOU	TAUGHT	MY
SIR 6:32	YOU	IF YOU	TAUGHT	BE	CAN	SON	MY	WISH
CAN	MY	TAUGHT	WISH	IF YOU	SON	SIR 6:32	BE	YOU
SON	WISH	BE	MY	YOU	SIR 6:32	TAUGHT	IF YOU	CAN

73

THOSE	LORD	4:14	HER	SIR	LOVE	WHO	THE	LOVES
WHO	LOVE	SIR	THE	LOVES	LORD	HER	THOSE	4:14
HER	LOVES	THE	WHO	4:14	THOSE	LORD	LOVE	SIR
4:14	THE	THOSE	LOVES	HER	SIR	LOVE	LORD	WHO
LOVES	WHO	HER	LOVE	LORD	4:14	THOSE	SIR	THE
LORD	SIR	LOVE	THOSE	THE	WHO	4:14	LOVES	HER
SIR	HER	LORD	4:14	LOVE	THE	LOVES	WHO	THOSE
THE	THOSE	LOVES	LORD	WHO	HER	SIR	4:14	LOVE
LOVE	4:14	WHO	SIR	THOSE	LOVES	THE	HER	LORD

74

LOVES	IT	IN	SIR 3:25	DANGER	HE	WILL	WHO	PERISH
WHO	DANGER	WILL	IT	PERISH	IN	HE	LOVES	SIR 3:25
HE	SIR 3:25	PERISH	WHO	LOVES	WILL	DANGER	IN	IT
DANGER	IN	LOVES	PERISH	HE	WHO	IT	SIR 3:25	WILL
SIR 3:25	HE	IT	LOVES	WILL	DANGER	WHO	PERISH	IN
WILL	PERISH	WHO	IN	SIR 3:25	IT	LOVES	HE	DANGER
IT	WHO	HE	WILL	IN	PERISH	SIR 3:25	DANGER	LOVES
PERISH	LOVES	DANGER	HE	IT	SIR 3:25	IN	WILL	WHO
IN	WILL	SIR 3:25	DANGER	WHO	LOVES	PERISH	IT	HE

75

BE	SIR	5:13	ANSWER	TO HEAR	TO	SLOW	BUT	SWIFT
ANSWER	SLOW	TO	5:13	BUT	SWIFT	TO HEAR	SIR	BE
BUT	TO HEAR	SWIFT	SLOW	BE	SIR	ANSWER	5:13	TO
TO	5:13	SIR	SWIFT	ANSWER	TO HEAR	BE	SLOW	BUT
TO HEAR	BUT	BE	TO	SLOW	5:13	SIR	SWIFT	ANSWER
SLOW	SWIFT	ANSWER	BUT	SIR	BE	TO	TO HEAR	5:13
SIR	TO	BUT	TO HEAR	5:13	ANSWER	SWIFT	BE	SLOW
SWIFT	BE	SLOW	SIR	TO	BUT	5:13	ANSWER	TO HEAR
5:13	ANSWER	TO HEAR	BE	SWIFT	SLOW	BUT	TO	SIR

76

A	WHO	PITIES	SNAKE	WHEN	CHARMER	SIR 12:13	HE IS	BITTEN
CHARMER	HE IS	WHEN	WHO	SIR 12:13	BITTEN	SNAKE	PITIES	A
BITTEN	SNAKE	SIR 12:13	HE IS	PITIES	A	WHO	CHARMER	WHEN
HE IS	A	CHARMER	SIR 12:13	WHO	SNAKE	WHEN	BITTEN	PITIES
WHEN	BITTEN	SNAKE	CHARMER	HE IS	PITIES	A	SIR 12:13	WHO
SIR 12:13	PITIES	WHO	A	BITTEN	WHEN	CHARMER	SNAKE	HE IS
PITIES	SIR 12:13	A	WHEN	SNAKE	HE IS	BITTEN	WHO	CHARMER
WHO	WHEN	BITTEN	PITIES	CHARMER	SIR 12:13	HE IS	A	SNAKE
SNAKE	CHARMER	HE IS	BITTEN	A	WHO	PITIES	WHEN	SIR 12:13

77

INTO	NOT	YOUR	11:29	MAN	SIR	EVERY	HOUSE	BRING
HOUSE	BRING	SIR	EVERY	INTO	YOUR	NOT	MAN	11:29
11:29	MAN	EVERY	HOUSE	NOT	BRING	SIR	INTO	YOUR
BRING	EVERY	HOUSE	MAN	YOUR	NOT	11:29	SIR	INTO
YOUR	SIR	INTO	BRING	HOUSE	11:29	MAN	NOT	EVERY
MAN	11:29	NOT	INTO	SIR	EVERY	BRING	YOUR	HOUSE
SIR	INTO	BRING	NOT	11:29	HOUSE	YOUR	EVERY	MAN
NOT	HOUSE	11:29	YOUR	EVERY	MAN	INTO	BRING	SIR
EVERY	YOUR	MAN	SIR	BRING	INTO	HOUSE	11:29	NOT

78

WITH	EVER	IS	ALLIED	A WOLF	A	SIR	13:16	LAMB
SIR	13:16	A WOLF	EVER	LAMB	IS	A	ALLIED	WITH
ALLIED	A	LAMB	WITH	SIR	13:16	A WOLF	IS	EVER
A WOLF	ALLIED	EVER	A	WITH	LAMB	IS	SIR	13:16
LAMB	SIR	WITH	IS	13:16	A WOLF	ALLIED	EVER	A
13:16	IS	A	SIR	ALLIED	EVER	LAMB	WITH	A WOLF
IS	A WOLF	ALLIED	LAMB	EVER	WITH	13:16	A	SIR
A	WITH	13:16	A WOLF	IS	SIR	EVER	LAMB	ALLIED
EVER	LAMB	SIR	13:16	A	ALLIED	WITH	A WOLF	IS

79

WILL	HE	FEARS	SIR 15:1	LORD	THIS	WHO	DO	THE
THE	THIS	DO	HE	WILL	WHO	LORD	SIR 15:1	FEARS
WHO	LORD	SIR 15:1	DO	THE	FEARS	THIS	WILL	HE
DO	SIR 15:1	THIS	THE	HE	LORD	WILL	FEARS	WHO
HE	WILL	LORD	WHO	FEARS	DO	THE	THIS	SIR 15:1
FEARS	THE	WHO	WILL	THIS	SIR 15:1	HE	LORD	DO
SIR 15:1	FEARS	WILL	LORD	WHO	HE	DO	THE	THIS
THIS	WHO	THE	FEARS	DO	WILL	SIR 15:1	HE	LORD
LORD	DO	HE	THIS	SIR 15:1	THE	FEARS	WHO	WILL

80

WHOEVER	HIS	14	DOES	SIR	REWARD	16:	GOOD	HAS
HAS	SIR	REWARD	WHOEVER	16:	GOOD	DOES	HIS	14
DOES	16:	GOOD	HAS	14	HIS	WHOEVER	SIR	REWARD
14	GOOD	WHOEVER	SIR	HAS	16:	REWARD	DOES	HIS
16:	DOES	HIS	14	REWARD	WHOEVER	SIR	HAS	GOOD
SIR	REWARD	HAS	GOOD	HIS	DOES	14	WHOEVER	16:
HIS	14	SIR	16:	DOES	HAS	GOOD	REWARD	WHOEVER
GOOD	HAS	DOES	REWARD	WHOEVER	14	HIS	16:	SIR
REWARD	WHOEVER	16:	HIS	GOOD	SIR	HAS	14	DOES

81

WHOSE	GRIEF	MOUTH	THE	SIR 14:1	BRINGS	NO	HIM	MAN
THE	NO	HIM	MAN	WHOSE	GRIEF	MOUTH	SIR 14:1	BRINGS
BRINGS	SIR 14:1	MAN	HIM	MOUTH	NO	WHOSE	THE	GRIEF
SIR 14:1	WHOSE	GRIEF	NO	BRINGS	HIM	MAN	MOUTH	THE
NO	MAN	THE	SIR 14:1	GRIEF	MOUTH	BRINGS	WHOSE	HIM
MOUTH	HIM	BRINGS	WHOSE	MAN	THE	SIR 14:1	GRIEF	NO
GRIEF	BRINGS	SIR 14:1	MOUTH	HIM	MAN	THE	NO	WHOSE
HIM	MOUTH	NO	BRINGS	THE	WHOSE	GRIEF	MAN	SIR 14:1
MAN	THE	WHOSE	GRIEF	NO	SIR 14:1	HIM	BRINGS	MOUTH

82

THAT	PATIENT	IS WHY	WITH	SIR 18:9	LORD	THE	IS	MEN
WITH	IS	MEN	IS WHY	PATIENT	THE	SIR 18:9	THAT	LORD
THE	LORD	SIR 18:9	THAT	IS	MEN	WITH	PATIENT	IS WHY
PATIENT	THE	THAT	MEN	IS WHY	IS	LORD	SIR 18:9	WITH
IS	IS WHY	WITH	THE	LORD	SIR 18:9	THAT	MEN	PATIENT
SIR 18:9	MEN	LORD	PATIENT	THAT	WITH	IS WHY	THE	IS
MEN	WITH	IS	SIR 18:9	THE	IS WHY	PATIENT	LORD	THAT
IS WHY	SIR 18:9	PATIENT	LORD	MEN	THAT	IS	WITH	THE
LORD	THAT	THE	IS	WITH	PATIENT	MEN	IS WHY	SIR 18:9

83

GIVE	SIR 17:20	AND	UP	TO	LORD	RETURN	THE	SIN
UP	TO	RETURN	SIN	THE	GIVE	LORD	SIR 17:20	AND
SIN	THE	LORD	AND	RETURN	SIR 17:20	UP	GIVE	TO
RETURN	LORD	SIN	SIR 17:20	GIVE	THE	AND	TO	UP
TO	UP	SIR 17:20	RETURN	AND	SIN	GIVE	LORD	THE
AND	GIVE	THE	LORD	UP	TO	SIR 17:20	SIN	RETURN
LORD	SIN	UP	TO	SIR 17:20	AND	THE	RETURN	GIVE
THE	RETURN	TO	GIVE	LORD	UP	SIN	AND	SIR 17:20
SIR 17:20	AND	GIVE	THE	SIN	RETURN	TO	UP	LORD

84

BLANDISHMENTS	VAIN	SIR	IN	THEIR	POUR	FORTH	20:12	FOOLS
POUR	IN	FOOLS	20:12	SIR	FORTH	VAIN	THEIR	BLANDISHMENTS
THEIR	FORTH	20:12	BLANDISHMENTS	FOOLS	VAIN	POUR	SIR	IN
SIR	20:12	POUR	FORTH	BLANDISHMENTS	THEIR	FOOLS	IN	VAIN
FORTH	FOOLS	THEIR	VAIN	IN	20:12	SIR	BLANDISHMENTS	POUR
VAIN	BLANDISHMENTS	IN	SIR	POUR	FOOLS	20:12	FORTH	THEIR
20:12	THEIR	VAIN	POUR	FORTH	IN	BLANDISHMENTS	FOOLS	SIR
IN	POUR	BLANDISHMENTS	FOOLS	20:12	SIR	THEIR	VAIN	FORTH
FOOLS	SIR	FORTH	THEIR	VAIN	BLANDISHMENTS	IN	POUR	20:12

85

VOICE	SIR	21:20	IN	RAISES	A	FOOL	LAUGHTER	HIS
RAISES	A	LAUGHTER	21:20	HIS	FOOL	VOICE	IN	SIR
IN	HIS	FOOL	LAUGHTER	VOICE	SIR	RAISES	A	21:20
SIR	VOICE	HIS	RAISES	A	21:20	IN	FOOL	LAUGHTER
21:20	LAUGHTER	IN	VOICE	FOOL	HIS	A	SIR	RAISES
FOOL	RAISES	A	SIR	LAUGHTER	IN	HIS	21:20	VOICE
LAUGHTER	IN	RAISES	A	21:20	VOICE	SIR	HIS	FOOL
HIS	21:20	SIR	FOOL	IN	RAISES	LAUGHTER	VOICE	A
A	FOOL	VOICE	HIS	SIR	LAUGHTER	21:20	RAISES	IN

86

OVER	WHO	SIR 22:27	MY	A	MOUTH	GUARD	SET	WILL
MOUTH	WILL	SET	GUARD	OVER	WHO	MY	SIR 22:27	A
MY	GUARD	A	WILL	SET	SIR 22:27	MOUTH	WHO	OVER
GUARD	OVER	MY	WHO	WILL	SET	A	MOUTH	SIR 22:27
WILL	A	WHO	SIR 22:27	MOUTH	MY	SET	OVER	GUARD
SET	SIR 22:27	MOUTH	A	GUARD	OVER	WILL	MY	WHO
WHO	SET	GUARD	OVER	MY	A	SIR 22:27	WILL	MOUTH
A	MOUTH	OVER	SET	SIR 22:27	WILL	WHO	GUARD	MY
SIR 22:27	MY	WILL	MOUTH	WHO	GUARD	OVER	A	SET

87

ALL	19:17	LORD	SIR	THE	IS	OF	WISDOM	FEAR
SIR	FEAR	WISDOM	OF	ALL	19:17	IS	THE	LORD
IS	OF	THE	LORD	WISDOM	FEAR	19:17	SIR	ALL
OF	WISDOM	SIR	IS	LORD	ALL	FEAR	19:17	THE
19:17	IS	FEAR	WISDOM	OF	THE	ALL	LORD	SIR
THE	LORD	ALL	FEAR	19:17	SIR	WISDOM	OF	IS
FEAR	THE	19:17	ALL	SIR	OF	LORD	IS	WISDOM
LORD	ALL	OF	THE	IS	WISDOM	SIR	FEAR	19:17
WISDOM	SIR	IS	19:17	FEAR	LORD	THE	ALL	OF

88

SIR	26:	3	A	GOOD	IS A	GENEROUS	WIFE	GIFT
IS A	GOOD	GIFT	3	GENEROUS	WIFE	SIR	A	26:
GENEROUS	A	WIFE	26:	SIR	GIFT	GOOD	3	IS A
26:	SIR	GENEROUS	WIFE	IS A	3	A	GIFT	GOOD
3	GIFT	GOOD	GENEROUS	26:	A	WIFE	IS A	SIR
A	WIFE	IS A	GOOD	GIFT	SIR	3	26:	GENEROUS
WIFE	GENEROUS	SIR	IS A	3	26:	GIFT	GOOD	A
GIFT	3	26:	SIR	A	GOOD	IS A	GENEROUS	WIFE
GOOD	IS A	A	GIFT	WIFE	GENEROUS	26:	SIR	3

89

TWO	SIR	MEN	23:	TYPES	OF	16	MULTIPLY	SINS
TYPES	OF	16	SIR	MULTIPLY	SINS	23:	TWO	MEN
SINS	MULTIPLY	23:	16	TWO	MEN	OF	SIR	TYPES
OF	TWO	TYPES	MULTIPLY	23:	SIR	MEN	SINS	16
MEN	16	SINS	TWO	OF	TYPES	SIR	23:	MULTIPLY
SIR	23:	MULTIPLY	MEN	SINS	16	TYPES	OF	TWO
16	TYPES	OF	SINS	SIR	TWO	MULTIPLY	MEN	23:
MULTIPLY	MEN	TWO	OF	16	23:	SINS	TYPES	SIR
23:	SINS	SIR	TYPES	MEN	MULTIPLY	TWO	16	OF

90

IN	NOT	YOUR	HAVE	YOU	SAVED	YOUTH	WHAT	SIR 25:3
YOUTH	WHAT	SIR 25:3	IN	YOUR	NOT	YOU	SAVED	HAVE
HAVE	YOU	SAVED	YOUTH	WHAT	SIR 25:3	YOUR	NOT	IN
NOT	YOUR	WHAT	SAVED	SIR 25:3	YOU	IN	HAVE	YOUTH
SIR 25:3	SAVED	IN	WHAT	HAVE	YOUTH	NOT	YOUR	YOU
YOU	YOUTH	HAVE	YOUR	NOT	IN	WHAT	SIR 25:3	SAVED
WHAT	SIR 25:3	YOU	NOT	IN	HAVE	SAVED	YOUTH	YOUR
YOUR	HAVE	YOUTH	YOU	SAVED	WHAT	SIR 25:3	IN	NOT
SAVED	IN	NOT	SIR 25:3	YOUTH	YOUR	HAVE	YOU	WHAT

91

AVOID	AND	WILL	YOUR	FEWER	STRIFE	SIR 28:8	SINS	BE
FEWER	BE	YOUR	AND	SINS	SIR 28:8	AVOID	STRIFE	WILL
SIR 28:8	SINS	STRIFE	BE	WILL	AVOID	FEWER	YOUR	AND
YOUR	STRIFE	SIR 28:8	AVOID	AND	BE	WILL	FEWER	SINS
AND	FEWER	SINS	SIR 28:8	YOUR	WILL	STRIFE	BE	AVOID
BE	WILL	AVOID	FEWER	STRIFE	SINS	AND	SIR 28:8	YOUR
SINS	SIR 28:8	FEWER	WILL	AVOID	YOUR	BE	AND	STRIFE
STRIFE	AVOID	BE	SINS	SIR 28:8	AND	YOUR	WILL	FEWER
WILL	YOUR	AND	STRIFE	BE	FEWER	SINS	AVOID	SIR 28:8

92

HARM	CAN	LORD	THE MAN	THE	SIR 33:1	WHO	NO EVIL	FEARS
THE MAN	THE	FEARS	NO EVIL	CAN	WHO	HARM	LORD	SIR 33:1
WHO	SIR 33:1	NO EVIL	FEARS	LORD	HARM	THE MAN	THE	CAN
CAN	NO EVIL	WHO	LORD	HARM	THE	SIR 33:1	FEARS	THE MAN
THE	FEARS	HARM	CAN	SIR 33:1	THE MAN	NO EVIL	WHO	LORD
SIR 33:1	LORD	THE MAN	WHO	NO EVIL	FEARS	THE	CAN	HARM
NO EVIL	HARM	SIR 33:1	THE	FEARS	LORD	CAN	THE MAN	WHO
FEARS	WHO	THE	HARM	THE MAN	CAN	LORD	SIR 33:1	NO EVIL
LORD	THE MAN	CAN	SIR 33:1	WHO	NO EVIL	FEARS	HARM	THE

www.ingramcontent.com/pod-product-compliance
Lightning Source LLC
Chambersburg PA
CBHW080935040426
42443CB00015B/3428